SCISSORS,

PAPER,

CRAFT

30 PRETTY PROJECTS ALL CUT, FOLDED, AND CRAFTED FROM PAPER

Christine Leech

BARRON'S

Photography by Keiko Oikawa

WHAT'S INSIDE?

CONTENTS

INTRODUCTION

I was so excited to be asked to do a papercraft book as paper is one of my favorite mediums to work in. My training as a graphic designer and illustrator gave me many excuses to play with paper: making giant collages from the teeniest scraps, bending and scoring thin cardboard into elaborate models, and sewing folded sheets into useful sketchbooks. The Rococo Mirror Frame on pages 98–101 is an updated version of some picture frames depicting architectural styles that I made for my Art Foundation course when I was 18, and I used to sell mini-notebooks like those on pages 38–41 at the school craft fair.

It's not just plain paper that I love. One of my favorite aromas is the smell of a freshly printed book and, more often than not, I sniff the pages before looking at what's printed on them (you do get some odd looks in bookshops). I also love collecting printed paraphernalia, from vintage bus tickets through German sausage packaging to American shop signage. My collection mostly sits in a box waiting for me to do something with it, but a few bits are scattered through this book and I'm glad to have found a use for them.

There's been a real boom in papercraft in recent years, with scrapbooking and card-making becoming many crafters' passions. The rise of these crafts has led to a miraculous increase in the type of papers, glues, decorations, and cutters you can buy, but this book only requires a few basic tools and a simple range of papers. There's a little something for everyone: if you are looking for unusual decorations for your party, make one or all of the various garlands in the book or try the Giant Gift Rosettes on pages 102–105. These would look brilliant at a baby shower or as a wedding backdrop and, speaking of weddings, the bouquet of crepe-paper anemones and camellias on pages 46–49 will last as long as your memories of the day.

I was on a ranch when I was commissioned to write this book, and the Colorado Critters on pages 14–17 were inspired by the wildlife I saw while there (though I only got first-hand experience of the deer and bison), as were the Feather Mobile on pages 86–89 and the Lifesize Cardboard Deer on pages 84–85.

Whatever you choose to make, have fun, enjoy it—and mind your fingers!

Christine

PAPERCRAFT KIT

I have a special metal pencil case that holds my favorite
craft knife, propelling pencil, metal ruler, and eraser.
Everything else lives in a jumble of a drawer. One day I will
have a beautifully organized craft room, but not today.

CUTTING THINGS

SCISSORS A variety of scissors will help you with your paper projects. You need large, sharp scissors that can cut through several sheets at a time, small scissors for delicate patterns, and a selection of pinking shears and decorative-edged scissors for ornate work. Don't mix up your fabric-cutting scissors with your paper-cutting ones. No good will come of it: your fabric scissors will go blunt from cutting paper and your paper scissors will not cut a nice straight edge of fabric.

KNIVES At college all our knives were surgical scalpels with 10A blades, and this is still the type I prefer. These days you can get many different knives, some with retractable, snap-off blades and some shaped like a pen so they are comfortable to hold. Find the knife you are most comfortable with and practice cutting straight lines and curves. ALWAYS cut on a cutting mat, not on your dining table. A utility or craft knife is good for cutting less intricate patterns as well as for cutting through thick cardboard and paper.

CUTTING MAT As I said, always use a cutting mat when using a knife. It provides a safe nonslip surface for your paper and is often made from self-healing plastic, so you can use it over and over again. Most mats have measurements marked out on them, which is handy. If the thing you are cutting is too big for a mat, then please make sure you have something underneath it that you don't mind getting scored.

PUNCHES From the simple office hole punch to the elaborate embossing and shaped punches, there are many different ways to cut paper shapes. In this book I have tried to limit the number of types of punches used, but if you have a hole punch, a 2" circle punch, and a 3¼" and a 2" flower-shaped punch, then you'll have everything you need. But don't worry if you don't have the shaped punches: you can cut the flower shapes with scissors—it will just take a little longer.

FIXING THINGS

STAPLER The projects in this book only require a simple stapler. I've always fancied one of those long-reach ones that can staple right into the middle of a book, but I haven't really got a use for it. A small stapler with little staples is also useful for tiny corners where a larger stapler may not fit.

SPRAY ADHESIVE Glue in a can. Great. Spray adhesive is great for covering areas of paper with a thin, even layer of glue. It can be permanent or repositionable. When spraying glue, always spray in a well-ventilated space and hold the can at least 8" from your paper. Move the can quickly and evenly across the area. If you are spraying thin paper, be careful not to spray for too long in one spot as the glue may seep through to the other side. When gluing paper shapes to a backing cardboard, spray the back of the paper shapes not the cardboard as some glues don't dry and you will be left with a sticky mess.

GLUE STICKS Good old glue sticks—one of the least messy forms of glue application. They are great for sticking paper and if you buy an extra-strength type, it is perfect for cardboard, too. You can buy glue sticks that go on colored and dry clear, which is useful if you only want to cover a particular area of paper as you can see what you're doing.

WHITE CRAFT GLUE This glue is also known as wood glue or PVA (which, fact fans, stands for Poly Vinyl Acetate). It is very strong, waterproof, and dries clear. Great for sticking large areas of cardboard and paper, it can be spread thinly with a spatula or small scrap of cardboard, and can also be watered down to make a more malleable, slower-drying glue that is useful for bookbinding. Dried white craft glue also peels off your hands like old skin.

GLUE DOTS Recently there has been a whole raft of new glue products that have made papercrafting much easier and less messy. Glue dots are one of these inventions. They come on a roll or on sheets in several different sizes. Choose from flat or raised dots, which give your work a nice three-dimensional quality.

GLUE SHEETS Glue sheets are a good substitute for spray adhesive if you just want to cover a small area. Basically, they are glue-covered sheets and when you place your paper on the glue, the glue transfers to your paper and gives it an adhesive back.

GLUE GUN Glue gun = fun. Hot glue guns and cold glue guns both melt glue sticks to give a quick-drying liquid adhesive that is great for sticking cardboard and decorations. The hot glue guns just melt the glue at a higher temperature and hotter glue burns more, so take care.

MASKING TAPE This beige papery tape is easy to tear, remove, and reposition. It stretches a little, which is useful when making cardboard hinges.

DOUBLE-SIDED TAPE I love double-sided tape. It is super-sticky but not messy and it fixes things instantly. Available in narrow or wide rolls, the narrow kind is the one I prefer. When I use the wide sort, I always find myself having to cut narrow strips from it!

WASHI TAPE A genius tape, with all the prettiness of beautiful Japanese rice papers, but with the sticking qualities of masking tape. Perfect for wrapping presents and fixing pictures to walls when you want something prettier than boring old clear tape or pins.

DUCT TAPE A strong, extremely sticky, cotton-based tape that tears easily when you have the knack—which I don't! Good for sticking large pieces of thick cardboard together.

MEASURING THINGS

RULERS When using a craft knife or scalpel, a metal ruler is a must. I have countless plastic rulers with nicks in them where the knife has veered dangerously and annoyingly into the ruler. It's useful to have both a 1 yard metal ruler—useful for measuring and cutting long, straight lengths—and a shorter metal ruler for the smaller projects. A small metal ruler is also good for making really crisp folds in paper. Just run the end of the ruler along the fold.

GEOMETRY SET A basic geometry set of compass, protractor, and right-angle drafting triangle will prove useful for many different things. If you can find a large right-angle drafting triangle, buy it as it will be invaluable when it comes to cutting squares.

DRAWING THINGS

DIP PEN AND INK Though a little messy (which is part of their charm), dip pens and india ink create a beautiful decorative effect. Alternatively, you can get many types of felt-tip pen with different nibs that give a variety of calligraphic and artistic lines.

MECHANICAL PENCIL Mechanical pencils are great; there is no need for pencil sharpeners as you'll always have a sharp point. But the thin lead of a mechanical pencil gives you much more accurate measuring points.

ERASER Though a sparkly strawberry-scented eraser might look (and smell) good, a simple white rubber eraser is preferable for removing unwanted pencil lines. Always clean your eraser on a spare piece of paper before you use it on your project.

OTHER THINGS

BRADAWL This tool, which is more often found in your toolbox, is good for making holes through cardboard or multiple sheets of paper. Always use it on top of an old piece of wood so you don't damage your table top.

COTTER PINS You can get lots of decorative cotter pins these days, so there's no need to use only the round, gold-colored ones. Craft shops sell packs in various colors and shapes. They are good for making hinges and for joining several pieces of paper together.

DECORATIVE ODDS AND ENDS Sequins, small buttons, adhesive gemstones, and glitter are all great for making your paper projects a little bit more special.

NEEDLES, THREADS, AND SEWING MACHINE Several projects in the book use a needle and thread, either to join pieces of paper together or to hang the final project. A variety of needle sizes will be useful and a sewing machine wouldn't go amiss either.

PAPER FACTS

There are lots of types of paper in the world and I like them all, whether it's the edible rice paper stuck on the bottom of a coconut macaroon or the giant, endless rolls of paper I see when I'm visiting a printing press.

PAPER WEIGHTS

Paper weights can be classed loosely as light, medium, and heavy (which includes thin cardboard). The weight is measured most understandably by the international standard of gsm—this is literally how many grams a square meter of the paper would weigh.

As a general rule, if you hold a piece of paper between your thumb and index finger and it droops, it's classified as lightweight, if there's a slight sag, then it's medium-weight, and if you can balance your cup of tea on it, then it's thick cardboard.*

LIGHTWEIGHT PAPER (35–90 GSM)
Tissue paper, newsprint, origami paper, photocopy and printer paper

MEDIUM-WEIGHT PAPER (105–165 GSM)
General letter paper, brown paper, pastel paper, light cardstock

HEAVYWEIGHT PAPER (175–335 GSM)
Watercolor paper and medium to heavy cardstocks (thin cardboards)—postcards, business cards, Bristol board

THICK CARDBOARD (400 GSM+)
Mounting and art board, gray bookbinding cardboard

PAPER SIZES

The most useful standard U.S. paper sizes for paper craft are: Letter or "A" (8½" x 11"), legal (8½" x 14"), ledger or "B" (11" x 17"), "C" (17" x 22"), and "D" (22" x 34"). But art papers can come in sundry sizes that don't necessarily match any "standard" sizes.

PAPER TYPES

Different papers are good for different things. I've used a variety of papers in this book. Here are some of my favorites.

TISSUE PAPER Often found wrapped around a pretty present, tissue paper is one of the thinnest papers you can find.

CREPE PAPER Crepe paper is perfect for making paper flowers as its stretch and strength allow you to curl petals and twist stems. Try to buy florist's crepe paper as it is much more durable than many art supply store versions. (See the Anemone and Camellia Bouquet, pages 46–49.)

TRANSLUCENT PAPER Not just the gray tracing paper of your school days. Now you can get see-through paper in a myriad of colors. Stronger than tissue paper, it is useful for stained-glass effects and for layering up different colors.

PRINTER PAPER Easy to come by and in loads of colors, printer paper is good for practicing on when trying out a project for the first time. I made prototypes of most of the projects in this book from white letter-size printer paper first.

ORIGAMI PAPER There are lots of different types of origami paper, ranging from traditional handmade and gilded to slick and shiny with modern designs. One- or two-sided, origami paper folds beautifully and has many uses beyond its traditional, historic one.

BROWN PACKAGING PAPER One of my favorite papers. I love the subtle lines embossed on it and its cheapness! Used in the right way it doesn't look cheap at all. (See the Rococo Mirror Frame, page 98–101.)

PASTEL PAPER Many projects in this book use pastel paper. It folds beautifully, comes in a wide range of colors, is nicely textured and ink doesn't bleed on it, so you can draw nice crisp lines on it. (See the Colorado Critters, pages 14–17.)

HANDMADE PAPER Handmade paper is especially beautiful as each sheet is unique. From paper that includes flower petals or sequins, to embossed, gold-leafed, hand-cut, and dyed, there are a million handmade papers to choose from. As the paper is made by hand, the fibers are not as "regimented" as in machine-made paper. This means it may not fold or tear as neatly as its factory-made counterpart.

WATERCOLOR PAPER This comes in several weights and has either a smooth or a rough texture. Some have a pretty deckled (feathered) edge that is the result of the manufacturing process.

CORRUGATED CARDBOARD This doesn't just come in brown rolls and sheets. You can get it in many colors. (See the Rustic Quilled Decorations, pages 90–93.)

WALLPAPER Wallpaper scraps or samples are great for projects that need either a more robust paper or long strips. The often oversized prints make it perfect for larger-scale projects. (See the Giant Gift Rosettes, pages 102–105.)

MOUNTING BOARD Mounting board is a nice sturdy art board often used, as the name suggests, for mounting work, be it your still-life exam pieces or your vacation photos. It comes in large and small sheets and in various sizes. Always buy the largest sheet you can as it is better value. If you're not anxious to cart large sheets around with you when out shopping or on the train home, some art shops will help you cut it down to a more manageable size. It is best cut with a craft or utility knife. (See the Pigeon Mail, pages 22–25.)

GRAY BOOKBINDING CARDBOARD This sad-looking board, often made from recycled fibers, is strong and perfect for bookbinding and for making boxes and folders. It comes in thicknesses ranging from 1 mm to 3 mm.

WORKING WITH PAPER

You don't need many supplies or specialist knowledge to make a successful paper project, but here are some tips for getting the best results.

PORTRAIT VERSUS LANDSCAPE

These are quite obvious terms for the way a paper rectangle is oriented. Paper that is wider than it is tall is landscape; if it is taller than it is wide, then it is portrait.

MAKING TEMPLATES

There are many templates at the back of this book and I recommend making cardboard templates from them. They will last longer and are easier to draw and cut around. If you have a computer and printer, you could scan the templates, enlarge them to the size you want on a photocopier, then print them in a pale color or at 20% of black on your chosen paper. If you trace the templates from the book, tape your tracing and your paper to your cutting mat and cut out both at once. This way you won't have pencil lines that will need erasing later.

PAPER GRAIN

Paper is made from fibers that are pulped together with water and dyes, then pressed and rolled flat. During this process, the fibers mostly lie down in one direction, which creates the grain of the paper. When you roll a piece of paper into a tube, you will be able to roll it more easily one way than the other. The easy way follows the way the grain is running. It is useful to know this as paper folds much more easily with the grain than against it. In bookbinding, make all your pages with the grain running parallel to the binding of the book; that way the pages won't become wavy.

ROLLING PAPER

If you are working on a project that requires tubes or cones (see the Colorado Critters, pages 14–17), then it helps if you warm up the paper first to relax the fibers in the grain. Start by finding the grain of the paper and roll a loose tube with the grain. Roll this tube back and forth on a table or between your hands for a while, then try to roll a tighter tube or cone. This way you will get a better effect and fewer creases in the paper.

If you have a large roll of paper that you want to lie flat, roll it out then roll it back on itself the other way. This encourages the fibers to lie flat. Ironing paper also helps but be careful, as heat can wrinkle some printed papers. Iron your chosen paper under a sheet of newsprint to protect your paper as well as the iron.

TEARING PAPER

Paper tears differently according to the grain and also according to the way you tear it. It tears much more easily and produces a straighter line if you tear with the grain rather than against it.

You also get different effects according to the way you hold and pull the paper. Imagine holding a portrait piece of paper in both hands. If you move your right hand toward you and your left away from you, you will get a different effect than if you pulled your left toward you and moved your right hand away. This is useful to know when deciding on the finish of tear you want on particular projects.

FOLDING PAPER

Again, paper folds better when working with the grain than against it, though this is less noticeable when using lightweight papers. To help fold heavier-weight papers, you can score along the foldline (see scoring paper, below) or fold against the edge of a ruler.

Many origami folds have special names. The most common ones used in this book are mountain fold and valley fold. Again, these are quite obvious terms—a mountain fold looks like a mountain and a valley one… yup, that's right.

To make your fold crisp, pinch it between your fingers and run your nails along it or place the paper on a flat surface and run the edge of a metal ruler or special folding tool along it.

SCORING PAPER

Scoring paper helps make folds crisper and neater and also helps you bend and fold curves inward. When I score paper I use the back (blunt) side of my craft knife and a metal ruler for straight lines or my free hand for doing curves (A). Don't dig the tip of the knife into the paper as it will drag; just press the long side of the blade firmly into the paper and pull. Be careful if you are scoring very thin paper as you can cut right through it.

Alternatively, you can use the blunt side of a pair of scissors. A dried-up ballpoint pen works well, too—though I always worry that it's going to come back to life and ruin my work. Remember to score on the correct side of the paper depending on whether you need a mountain or a valley fold.

After scoring a curve, pick the paper up and pinch it gently between your fingers to persuade the paper to curve (B).

CUTTING PAPER

Paper can be cut using scissors or a knife. I prefer a knife as the cut is much more accurate. Ideally, if you are working with medium-weight to heavyweight paper, you should change the blade of your knife for each new project or change it a couple of times while working on the project.

If you are working on a small delicate papercut, it is sometimes easiest to attach the paper (and the template, if using) to the cutting mat with masking tape to secure it.

Always cut the inside lines of the pattern first and the lines of the exterior/outline shape last. And don't try to cut too much of the design in one go. Do little sections at a time and go slowly. If you're cutting a curvy shape from cardboard or thick paper, cut small sections away rather than trying to cut a big curve all at once.

CURLING PAPER

Several projects call for curled paper. Curl the paper by holding the paper strip in one hand and running a closed pair of scissors along its length. The paper will curl when you reach the end. A firmer pull gives a tighter curl (C and D).

COLORADO CRITTERS

ᴧᴧᴧᴧᴧᴧᴧᴧᴧᴧᴧᴧᴧᴧᴧᴧᴧᴧᴧᴧᴧᴧᴧᴧᴧᴧᴧᴧᴧ

Last summer I vacationed at the beautiful Zapata Ranch in Colorado. These paper animals were inspired by some of the creatures I saw while I was there. To be fair, I didn't actually see a bear or a wolf or a snow fox, but I definitely saw deer!

SUPPLIES

Letter-size sheets of medium-weight paper in various colors

Pencil

Scissors

Craft knife and cutting mat

Metal ruler

Pin

makes 1 set of critters

All these critters are made in the same way; the only difference is how you fold their necks and tails.

TO MAKE MOMMA BEAR

1. Fold a letter-size sheet of paper in half lengthwise. Using the template on page 115, place the template on the paper with the top edge along the foldline. Trace around the template with a sharp pencil, making small marks on the bear's neck at the crease lines.

2. Using scissors, cut out the bear just inside the pencil line. That way there will be fewer pencil marks to erase later. Using a craft knife, cut out the bear's ears.

3. Using the blunt back edge of the craft knife and a metal ruler, score the two crease lines across the bear's neck.

4. Fold the bear along both the scored lines. Run your fingernails along the scored lines to crease firmly.

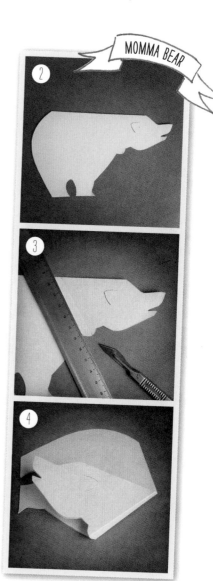

MOMMA BEAR

CONT. 〉〉〉

5. Open out the bear and make an inverse fold on her head at the line marked fold A; push her head down and in-between her front paws.

6. Holding onto the bear's back, just behind fold A, mountain fold her head out from between her paws along fold B.

7. Using a pin, push in the point to make the bear's eyes.

8. Using the template on page 115, trace and cut out the fish from a different color and place in Momma Bear's mouth.

TO MAKE BABY BEAR

Baby Bear is made in exactly the same way as Momma Bear using the templates from page 115 but, as his neck creases are in slightly different positions, his neck reaches upward instead of staying straight.

MOMMA BEAR

TO MAKE MOMMA DEER

1. Follow Momma Bear steps 1–8 using the template on page 114.

2. To make the deer's tail reach upward, score a line at the point marked fold C, then open her body out flat and fold up her tail. Close her body again and her tail will automatically fold over her back. You can also fold her antlers for added character.

3. Don't forget to make her eyes with a pin.

TO MAKE BABY DEER

The Baby Deer template looks slightly odd as her head is upside down, but all will become clear when you fold her neck.

1. Follow Momma Bear steps 1–3 using the template on page 114. Score Baby Deer's neck line and fold her neck flat to one side.

2. Open Baby Deer out, then inverse-fold her neck between her front hooves.

3. Fold Baby Deer flat again and her head will be the right way up so she can sniff around in the grass looking for treats.

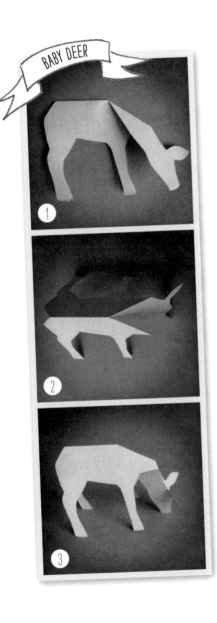

BABY DEER

1

2

3

TO MAKE SNOW FOX

1. Follow Momma Bear steps 1–3 using the template on page 114.

2. Snow Fox's neck is folded in the same way as Baby Deer's.

3. For his tail, make an inverse fold between his hind legs so his tail points straight down.

4. Next, make a second inverse fold so his tail points out to the side.

TO MAKE WOLFIE

1. Follow Momma Bear steps 1–3 using the template on page 114.

2. Wolfie's neck is folded in the same way as Baby Bear's.

3. Wolfie's tail is folded in the same way as Momma Deer's.
If you prefer the tail not to lay flat, adjust the fold.

TO MAKE THE BISON FAMILY

The Bison Family are made in the exactly the same way as the Bear Family.

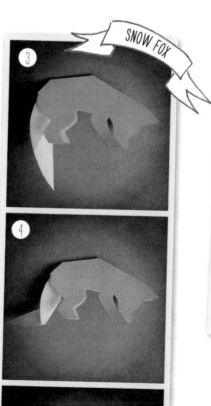

SNOW FOX

3

4

BIRDHOUSE DESK TIDY

A sticky-note dispenser and paperclip holder in the shape of a birdhouse. What more could you want?

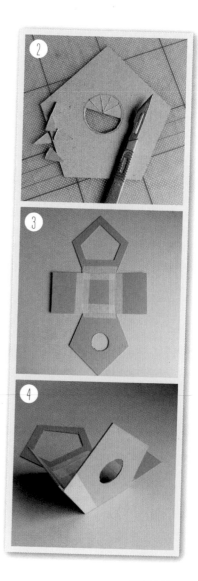

TO MAKE THE BIRDHOUSE

1. Using the templates on pages 116–117, trace and cut out the birdhouse front and back from the cardboard. Then cut one 2³⁄₄" x 2¹⁄₂" rectangle for the base and two 2³⁄₄" x 2¹⁄₄" rectangles for the sides.

2. Cut out the circular entrance on the birdhouse front. The easiest way to do this is to cut lots of straight lines across the circle, all crossing in the middle, then cut away each wedge-shaped segment in turn. (The hole will eventually be covered, so it doesn't need to be super-neat.)

3. Place the two birdhouse sides on either side of the base so edges of the same length touch. Use masking tape to join them together. The masking tape will act as a hinge so the sides will be able to fold up. Secure the front and back of the birdhouse to the remaining sides of the base with masking tape.

4. Fold up one side and the front of the birdhouse so their edges touch and use masking tape to fix them in place (it's easier to place the masking tape on the outside of the box at this point).

CONT. >>>

SUPPLIES

11³⁄₄" x 16¹⁄₂" piece of 3mm-thick gray cardboard

Craft knife

Metal ruler

Cutting mat

Masking tape

White craft glue

Double-sided tape

Selection of brightly colored papers in plains or prints (I used origami paper)

Glue stick

Pack of bright pink sticky notes

Circle cutter

makes 1

5. Repeat with the other side of the birdhouse and then fold up the back to create a roofless box. To reinforce the birdhouse sides, run a little white craft glue along the inside joints and leave to dry.

TO COVER THE BIRDHOUSE

6. Cover the front of the birdhouse with strips of double-sided tape, then peel away the protective backing. (Double-sided tape fixes the paper firmly in place but also makes the box more rigid. You can use glue but this can get messy and doesn't hold the paper in place instantly.)

7. Place a piece of origami paper right side down on a flat surface, then place the birdhouse, sticky side down, on top. Use scissors to cut away the excess paper, leaving a ³/₈" border all around.

8. Repeat with the back of the box. To cut the opening, run the craft knife from the corners to the center of the hole and cut away the excess paper, leaving a ³/₈" border along each edge. Fold this paper into the hole to create a neat edge. Repeat at the front.

9. Fold the excess paper into the box, creasing or cutting the paper at the corners to make them neater. Use double-sided tape or a glue stick to glue the excess to the inside of the box.

10. Cover the three outer sides of the box with a glue stick. Cut a 3" x 8¼" rectangle of origami paper. Place it on the box with a ³/₈" allowance, starting at one side then pressing it onto the glue over the base and up the other side. Try to keep the edges of the paper flush with the front and back of the box. Fold over the two short ends of paper into the box.

TO LINE THE BOX

11. Using the templates again on pages 116–117, cut out the front, back, base, and sides from origami paper. Cut away the paper to create the openings on the front and back.

12. Cover the inside of the box with a glue stick, then stick the pieces in place. Start with the front and back, then the base and finally the sides. Press down firmly and leave to dry.

TO MAKE THE ROOF

13. Cut two 3¼" x 3½" rectangles of gray cardboard for the roof. Place one short side of each card piece together so they are almost touching, then join with a strip of masking tape. Run a second piece of masking tape over the other side of the join to reinforce it. The roof must hinge in the center so it sits neatly on top of the birdhouse.

14. To cover the roof, run a length of double-sided tape all around the rectangle on the upper side of the roof.

15. Place a 4" x 8" rectangle of origami paper right side down. Place the cardboard, sticky side down, on the origami paper, trimming the paper as shown for neat corners. Fold over the edges of the paper and glue in place on the underside.

16. Cut six strips ¼" x 3¼" of double-sided tape and place them all around the top of the birdhouse along the very edge of the cardboard.

17. Place the roof on top of these strips and press it firmly in place. It's best if there is a slight overhang at the front of the birdhouse and the rear is flush with the back. Split the pad of sticky notes in two and use double-sided tape to fix each half to the roof.

18. Use a circle cutter to make a ring from white paper for the front entrance. Make the outer hole 1½" and the inner one 1". Glue this to the front of the box over the hole.

19. Hang your birdhouse from a hook on a bulletin board or sit it on your desk. You'll never be at a loss for sticky notes and you'll always have somewhere to store your paper clips and office odds and ends.

PIGEON MAIL

These well-dressed little pigeons do a great job of keeping all your mail and important bits of paper neat and tidy. Fix them to your wall or bulletin board for an organized life.

SUPPLIES

6" x 8¼" piece of colored mounting board

Cutting mat

Craft knife

Selection of colored pastel papers in 4", 3", and 2" squares

Dip pen and black ink or black calligraphy pen

Double-sided tape

Scraps of colored paper for eyes and accessories

Hole punch

makes 1

TOP TIP

If you have only one color of mounting board, using spray adhesive, stick different-colored paper over the board to create different-colored birds.

TO MAKE THE PIGEONS

1. Using the templates on pages 116–117, trace the pigeon outlines onto the reverse of the mounting board.

2. Lay the mounting board on the cutting mat and, using a craft knife, cut out the pigeons. As the pigeons are quite curvy in shape, the easiest way to achieve a neat finish is it to cut away small pieces at a time. Do not try to cut an entire curve at once.

TO MAKE THE PIGEONS' WINGS

3. Cut the curve of the pigeon's wing slit between marked points A and B.

CONT. >>>

4. Using the wing templates on page 116, trace the three different-sized wings onto the three different-colored pastel papers. Using the dip pen and ink or calligraphy pen, draw a curly line to accentuate the scalloped edge of each wing.

5. Once the ink is dry, cut out each wing piece and stick a strip of double-sided tape along the top edge on the reverse side.

6. Layer the wing pieces on top of each other to build up the wing. Remove the protective backing from the tape and stick down the small and medium-size wing pieces. Finally, stick the entire wing onto the pigeon body so it covers up the wing slit.

Now accessorize each pigeon in a different way.

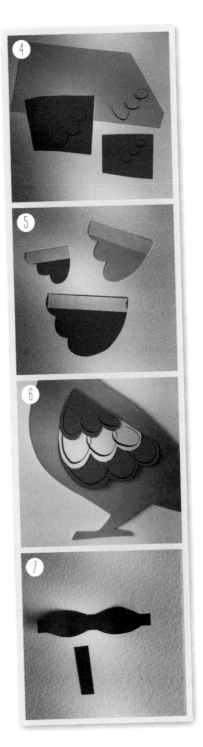

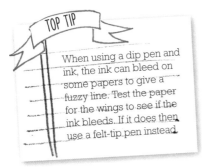

TOP TIP

When using a dip pen and ink, the ink can bleed on some papers to give a fuzzy line. Test the paper for the wings to see if the ink bleeds. If it does then use a felt-tip pen instead.

TO MAKE THE BOW TIE

7. To make the bow tie, using the templates on page 116, trace and cut out the two bow tie pieces. Fold the body of the bow tie where indicated then fold the center of the tie around the body. Fix the tie in place on the reverse with a little double-sided tape. Using the dip pen and ink, draw a bow tie shape onto the paper bow tie.

TO MAKE THE EYES AND OTHER ACCESSORIES

8. Cut out a small oval for each eye and, using a hole punch, create a perfect circle for the pupils.

9. Using a hole punch, make a selection of paper buttons and necklaces. To make the headpiece, follow the instructions for the roses on page 55.

Selection of pieces of patterned wallpaper and colored paper

Craft knife or scissors

3 mm-thick gray cardboard in the following sizes:

SMALL BOX

Four 4³/₄" x 4³/₄" squares

One 4³/₄" x 4⁵/₈" rectangle

LARGE BOX

Four 9" x 7" rectangles

One 9" x 6⁷/₈" rectangle

RECTANGULAR BOX

Two 11" x 4³/₄" rectangles

Two 4³/₄" x 4³/₄" squares

One 11" x 4⁵/₈" rectangle

(You will notice that the base of the box is very slightly smaller than the four sides. This allows the base to fit snugly between the sides.)

LARGE TRIANGLE

Two 3¹/₄" x 10" rectangles

One 3¹/₄" x 4" rectangle

SMALL TRIANGLE

Two 7" x 5" rectangles

One 5" x 5" square

Craft knife

Double-sided tape

Masking tape

Pencil

Glue stick

makes 1 of each

DOLLHOUSE STORAGE SYSTEM

Is it a dollhouse? Certainly! Is it a church? Could be! Is it a nifty bit of storage for your home office? Oh yeah, it's that, too!

TO MAKE THE SMALL BOX

1. Cut a 6¹/₄" square of colored paper. Place it colored side down on a flat surface. Put the 4³/₄" x 4⁵/₈" rectangle of cardboard in the middle of the square. Attach lengths of double-sided tape along each edge of the cardboard. Cut away the corners of the paper as shown and remove the tape's protective backing.

2. Fold one edge of the paper over onto the cardboard and press it onto the double-sided tape to create a neat corner.

3. Fold the adjacent edge of paper onto the cardboard. Repeat until all the edges have been folded in and secured.

CONT. >>>

》》》

4. Use masking tape to attach each of the four square sides of the box to the base. Masking tape allows you to reposition the pieces if necessary and it stretches as you fold the sides of the box up.

5. Fold the sides of the box up one by one. As you fold them up, use masking tape to join two adjacent sides together at the corner (5A).

The corners should abut each other as shown (5B).

6. When you fold up the fourth side, it should fit snugly between the sides of the box and the slightly smaller base.

7. Reinforce all the joins with more masking tape.

TO COVER THE BOX

8. Stand the box in the center of a piece of patterned wallpaper, print side down and large enough to cover all sides (approximately 16" square). Draw around the base of the box with a pencil. Tip the box onto one of its sides and draw around the side. Tip it back to the center then down onto another side. Repeat until you have a penciled

outline of all four sides and the base. Remove the box.

9. Add a ³⁄₄" border at the top of two opposite sides and a ³⁄₄" border on three edges of the remaining two opposite sides. Use scissors or a knife to cut out the paper. Trim each corner at an angle as in step 1.

10. Attach lengths of double-sided tape along each of the four edges of the base of the box, then stand the box in the center of the paper, pressing firmly so it sticks to the paper.

EXTRA!

Instead of using double-sided tape to attach the paper to the box, you could use white craft glue. It allows for repositioning of the paper but it is more messy!

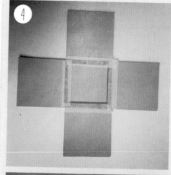

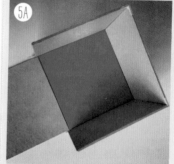

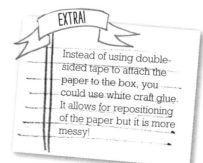

11. To cover the first two opposite sides of the box with paper, tip the box down again onto one of the sides of paper with the three extra flaps (11A). With the box still lying down, attach double-sided tape to the box along the two sides and the inside edge of the open top. Fold the flaps onto the tape and press firmly (11B). Repeat on the opposite side. (To keep the paper nice and flat, it is best to keep the box on the table and roll the two opposite sides down in turn onto the paper. This works better than folding the paper up over the side.)

12. With the box sitting on its base, attach double-sided tape along the edges of one of the uncovered sides, on top of the colored paper flaps. This time, fold the paper up over the side and press it down to stick it in place. Repeat on the opposite side. Fix the top edges of paper inside the box with double-sided tape.

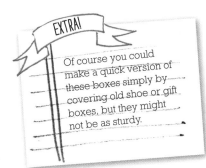

EXTRA!

Of course you could make a quick version of these boxes simply by covering old shoe or gift boxes, but they might not be as sturdy.

13. To cover the inside of the box, cut four $4\frac{5}{8}$" squares from the same paper as you used on the inside base.

14. Cover each of the inside faces of the box with glue stick and glue one of the squares of paper to each face.

15. Make the large and rectangular boxes in the same way. The triangles are made similarly, but it is easiest to make the cardboard triangle first, then cover it with paper and finally cut rectangles of lining paper to cover the inside.

5" x 11½" rectangle of medium-weight turquoise paper

Metal ruler

Pencil

Cutting mat

Craft knife

5" square of medium-weight ivory paper

Spray adhesive

Masking tape (optional)

Glue sheets (optional)

Scraps of plain and patterned colored papers for the birds and banner

¾" x 6½" strip of medium-weight turquoise paper

Glue stick

Dressmaking pin

Double-sided tape

makes 1

BIRDCAGE POP-UP CARD

When I was 11, I had a birthday card from my aunt that had a beautiful house on it whose windows and doors all opened. I used it for years after as a kind of Advent calendar countdown for my birthday. This card is partially inspired by that one.

EXTRA!

It's good to use temporary glue when fixing the birds to their hinges, then you can make sure you get them in just the right position before fixing them more securely.

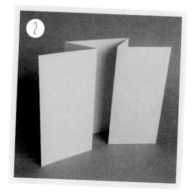

TO MAKE THE BASE CARD

1. Make a small mark at the center of one long side of the 5" x 11½" rectangle of turquoise paper. Measure and mark 1½" to the right from this center point, then measure another 1½" to the right and make a third mark. Repeat to the left of the center mark to make two more marks. Repeat on the opposite long side of the turquoise rectangle.

2. Place the rectangle on the cutting mat and, ignoring the center mark, use the craft knife and metal ruler to score four straight lines between the marks, then crease the rectangle along the scored lines.

CONT. >>>

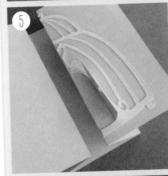

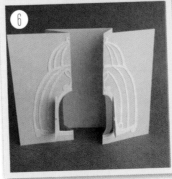

»»

3. Copy the template on page 118 and attach it to the ivory paper either with a light spray of spray adhesive or with masking tape around the edges. Cut out the birdcage. (See page 13 for hints on cutting paper.) When cutting the doors, leave the hinge area intact.

4. Cut the birdcage in two down the center. Score the door hinges so the doors can open and close.

5. Place one half of the birdcage on the creased turquoise rectangle, making sure that the edge of the birdcage lines up with the crease, as shown. Lift the door and pencil lightly around the door frame onto the turquoise paper below. Repeat with the other half of the birdcage.

6. Cut away the turquoise paper around the door frame. Attach the halves of the birdcage to the front of the turquoise paper using either spray adhesive or glue sheets.

TO MAKE THE BIRDS AND BANNER

7. Using the templates on page 118, cut the birds, wings, and banner from the plain and patterned papers.

8. To make the banner three-dimensional, score and fold where shown. Fold lines A away from you and lines B toward you.

9. Cut the 3/4" x 6½" strip of turquoise paper in half lengthwise. Score four lines each 3/8" apart from the next at one end of each of the strips.

10. Use a glue stick to lightly glue Bird 1 to the unscored end of one of 3¼" strips so its beak just overlaps the end.

11. Glue the banner onto the strip, under the bird's beak and overlapping its body. Glue the wing to the bird and make an eye with a pin.

12. Place a little double-sided tape or glue on the first scored square of the strip, then fold it up into a cube and fix it in place, as shown.

13. Glue Bird 2 to the second strip, then repeat step 12 and add a wing and make an eye. Place

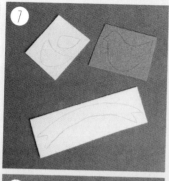

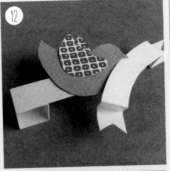

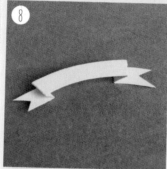

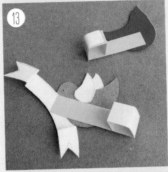

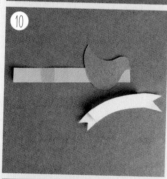

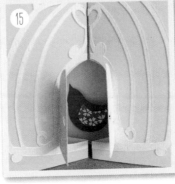

double-sided tape on the back and side of each bird's cube.

14. Remove the protective backing from the double-sided tape and place Bird 1 and its banner on the inside of the card so that one face of the cube is attached to the back of the card and one is attached to the side flap.

15. Repeat with Bird 2, making sure you can see the bird through the door when the card is closed.

16. Using the templates from page 118, cut flowers from patterned papers, then stick to the inside of the card.

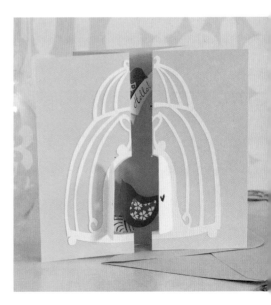

BIRD AND NAME GARLAND

This simple little card gives the recipient a lovely surprise when they open it and pull a long string of letters from the envelope.

CONT. >>>

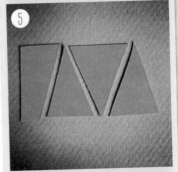

Pencil

White paper

Scissors

Spray adhesive

One 4" square of decorative paper per letter

One 4" square of thin colored cardboard per letter, plus one for the bird

Masking tape

Cutting mat

Craft knife

Scraps of colored paper for bunting and bird's wing

Large-eyed needle

Embroidery thread

Glue stick

Large luggage tag

Envelope

1. Start by making the name template. Either write your chosen name freehand on white paper or print out the name using a computer font, making each letter about 4" tall.
You can get lots of free decorative fonts online (see Resources on page 126 for websites). Cut out the name into its individual letters.

2. For each letter, use spray adhesive to stick together one square of decorative paper and one square of thin colored cardboard. Choose attractive combinations of paper and cardboard. Lay the template of one of the letters on top of the doubled-up square. Fix it in place with some masking tape, then attach the two pieces to your cutting mat with masking tape top and bottom.

3. Carefully cut out the letter with a craft knife.

4. Repeat steps 2 and 3 for each letter.

makes 1

5. To make the bunting, use the template on page 122 to cut the triangles from paper (or thin cardboard).

6. Using the templates on page 122, cut out the bird pieces.

7. Thread a large-eyed needle with embroidery thread long enough to attach the whole name and the bunting. Sew the bird onto the thread through the holes marked on the template, leaving about 4" of thread for hanging. Cover the thread by gluing the wing over it with glue stick.

8. Sew bunting triangles alternating with letters onto the thread and finish off by tying on the luggage tag.

9. Write your message on the luggage tag, then carefully concertina the garland into an envelope.

EXTRA!

Instead of a name you could spell out congratulations or happy birthday or even the date of a special occasion.

Happy birthday, Lovely

JAPANESE-BOUND NOTEBOOKS

These notebooks are made from one large sheet of watercolor paper folded to make the leaves of the book. Their size makes them ideal to carry around with you to use as sketchbooks or to make notes when inspiration strikes.

SUPPLIES

22" x 30" sheet of medium-weight (135 gsm) watercolor paper

Two bulldog clips

Right-angle drafting triangle

Pencil

Craft knife and cutting mat

Metal ruler

Drill with 2 mm drill bit (or bradawl)

Block of old wood, for drilling

Large needle

1 yd of colored butcher's string (or thin ribbon)

makes 1

TO MAKE THE BASIC BOOK BLOCK

1. Lay the sheet of paper landscape format on a clean, flat surface. Fold the paper into sixteenths, this will take four folds.
Fold 1: fold in half widthwise.
Fold 2: fold in half from top to bottom.
Fold 3: fold in half widthwise again.
Fold 4: fold in half from top to bottom again. Depending on the thickness of your paper, folds 3 and 4 may prove tough but a good, hard squash will help. You now have your basic book block with a spine and 16 pages, some of which are joined at the folds.

2. Next, you need to release the joined pages. First hold the book closed by placing bulldog clips along the long rough edge opposite the spine.

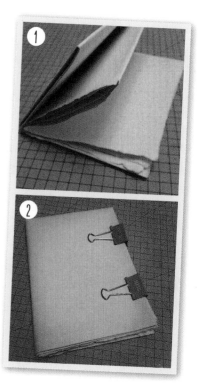

CONT. >>>

3. Using the set square placed against the spine, draw a faint pencil line 3/16" in from the top edge of the pages. Repeat along the long edge. For the second short edge, measure and mark a line 6⅞" from the line at the top edge. (You will find it easier if you move the bulldog clips around as you mark the lines.)

4. Using a metal ruler and craft knife, neatly trim the pages along the pencil lines. (Again, move the bulldog clips as you trim each side.) You now have an 6⅞" tall notebook of 16 pages.

5. Return the bulldog clips to the long edge of the notebook, opposite the spine. Referring to the appropriate guide on pages 118–119, use a metal ruler and pencil to mark the holes where indicated on the guide. Place a block of wood underneath the book block and use a drill and drill bit to make small holes at the marked points.

EXTRA

Decorate the cover of your book with rubber stamps, hand-lettering or pieces of patterned paper. If you want to add a patterned paper cover, wrap a sheet of paper around the book block before step 3, then trim it along with the book pages to the same size before continuing to follow the rest of the instructions.

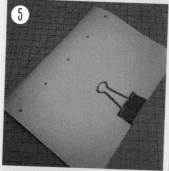

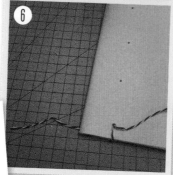

TO MAKE THE BOOK WITH RED BINDING

6. Thread the needle with string and, starting at the bottom, begin binding the book together as follows:

Enter hole A from the rear of the book. Leaving a 3¼" tail end of string, take the string around the base of the book and back into hole A from the rear.

Take the string around the spine of the book and back into hole A from the rear.

Enter hole B from the front, take the string around the spine and back into hole B from the front.

Enter hole C from the rear, take the string around the spine and back into hole C from the rear.

Enter hole D from the front, take the string around the spine and back into hole D from the front.

Enter hole E from the rear, take the string around the spine and back into hole E from the rear.

Take the string around the top of the book and back into hole E from the rear.

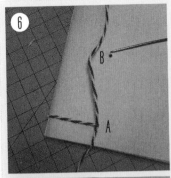

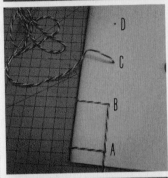

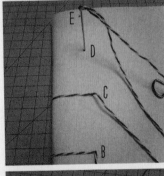

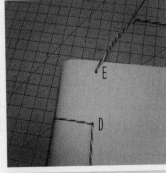

7. Travel back down the book spine, stitching from hole E to D at the front of the book, hole D to C at the back of the book, and hole C to B at the front of the book.

8. To finish off the binding, tie a knot at the rear of the book between holes A and B.

9. Once you've made this book, you can make the brown and the blue books using the stitch guides on pages 118–119.

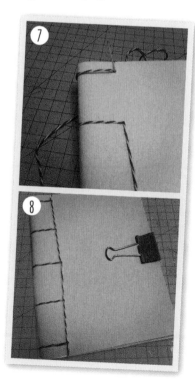

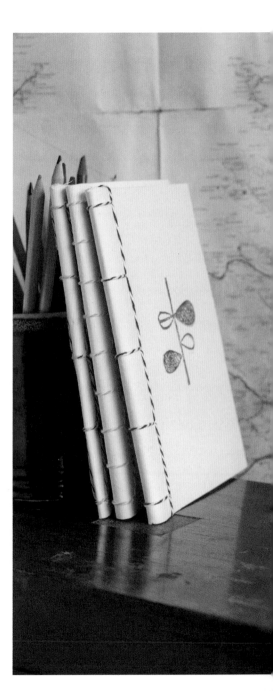

EXTRA!

The fibers in handmade paper are thick and long, which means that it is more flexible and malleable, and less likely to tear at the creases on the covers of this book.

WEDDING GUEST BOOK

Two letter-size pads (not spiral-bound) of thin watercolor paper backed with thick gray cardboard

Craft knife and cutting mat

Metal ruler

Double-sided tape

Two rectangles of differently patterned handmade paper, 1¼" larger all around than the watercolor paper

Pencil

Masking tape

Glue stick

Decorative-edged scissors

Two pieces of brown packaging paper, the same size as the watercolor paper

Spray adhesive (optional)

Bulldog clip

Two ¾" screw posts

Block of old wood, for drilling

Drill and drill bit the same size as the screw posts

Screwdriver (optional)

White craft glue

Small envelopes

makes 1

I've made several of these for my friends' weddings. A guest book is lovely to give as a gift, but keep it with you throughout the day and get all the guests to sign their name and add a little message. The envelopes dotted throughout the book are good for storing keepsakes and if you can get your hands on an instant camera to add some photos, then that's all the more fun!

TO MAKE THE BOOK'S COVER

1. Separate the pads of watercolor paper from their covers but keep the backing cardboard for the book's front and back covers. Separate the individual sheets of paper. Remove any excess glue from the spine edge of the paper.

2. Place one of the pieces of thick cardboard on the cutting mat and use a craft knife and ruler to cut a ³⁄₁₆" strip off one of the short sides. Discard the strip. Measure and cut off a 1¼" strip from the same short side so you now have a larger and a smaller piece. Attach a strip of ³⁄₈"-wide double-sided tape along one short side of the larger piece of cardboard and another along one long side of the smaller piece of cardboard. Set these aside.

3. Center the uncut piece of thick cardboard on the wrong side of one of the rectangles of patterned paper.

Draw around the cardboard, then remove. Remove the protective backing from the double-sided tape on the cut pieces of cardboard and place the two pieces of cardboard, tape side down, on the drawn rectangle so their short sides butt up to the lines. Having cut away the ³⁄₁₆" strip in step 2, there will be a gap of ³⁄₁₆" between the two pieces. This will form the hinge for the front cover of the book.

CONT. >>>

4. Cut all four corners of the paper at an angle, leaving approximately $1/8$" near the corners of the card. Attach strips of double-sided tape along all four sides of the cardboard, right along the edge.

5. Starting at the top, long side of the cardboard, remove the backing from the tape and gently pull the flap of paper down onto it, pressing firmly to stick it down all around.

6. Repeat at the adjacent short side. Where the paper overlaps at the corner, tuck the little extra piece of paper into the fold to hide it. Repeat on the two other sides of the cardboard.

TO MAKE THE BOOK'S SPINE

7. Cut a $4^3/4$" x $10^1/2$" rectangle from the other rectangle of patterned paper. Place the rectangle, patterned side down, on a flat surface and run a length of double-sided tape along its long left-hand edge. Lay the front cover of the book on top so the patterned paper overlaps the main part of the cover by $5/8$". The spine also reinforces the hinge.

8. Attach a short length of masking tape along the inside edge of the cover and fold the top edge of the spine down onto it (8A). Fold the rest of the top edge of the spine at a slight angle (8B) and cover the remainder of the spine with glue stick. Pull the glued spine onto the cover of the book and press it in place.

9. While the glue is still drying, gently fold the hinge back and forth a couple of times to allow the paper to stretch naturally over the hinged area. Keep pressing the paper flat as you do this and it will settle into place.

10. Repeat steps 4–8 with the other piece of thick cardboard to make the back cover.

TO FINISH THE BOOK

11. To hide the raw edges on the inside of the covers, use the decorative-edged scissors to trim the two pieces of brown paper to $3/8$" smaller all around than the watercolor paper. Cover the back of each of the pieces of brown paper with glue stick or spray adhesive and press them in place on the inside of the covers.

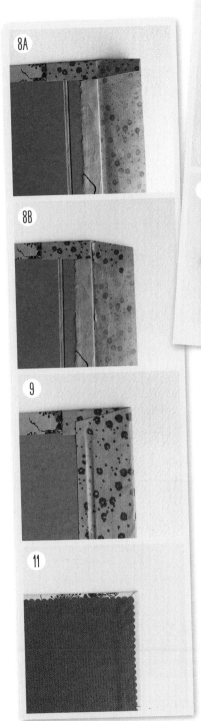

8A

8B

9

11

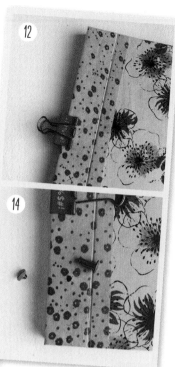

12

14

14. Push the long part of a screw post through one of the drilled holes from the front. Screw the short part into the post and tighten with a screwdriver if necessary. Repeat with the other post.

15. Glue pretty envelopes onto pages throughout the book for guests to use to hold their little souvenirs of the day. You can also leave notepaper and luggage tags on tables or by the book so people can write messages to add to the book later.

12. Sandwich the pieces of watercolor paper between the front and back covers and line them up so all the edges are neat. Hold them together with a bulldog clip. Mark the positions of the screw posts on the spine, $5/8$" in from the edge and 2" from the top and bottom.

13. Place the book on the piece of wood. Using a drill bit to match the diameter of the screw post and holding the book firmly to stop it spinning around with the drill, drill a hole through one of the pencil marks. Repeat for the other pencil marks.

ANEMONE AND CAMELLIA BOUQUET

Nothing quite matches the beauty of real flowers but these paper versions of two of my favorite flowers make a quirky and long-lasting bouquet for any bride. Using a cupcake pan ensures the flowers hold their beautiful curved shape.

Pencil

Thin cardboard, for template

Scissors

Florist's crepe paper in white, black, and lime green

Cupcake pan

White craft glue

Pinking shears

Ten 3/4" paper or polystyrene balls

6" diameter polystyrene ball

Small bowl or mug

Pearl-headed pins

8" of grosgrain ribbon

makes 1

TO MAKE THE ANEMONES

1. Copy the anemone petal template from page 120 onto thin cardboard.

2. Cut six rectangles of white crepe paper just larger than the template. Layer them on top of each other, making sure the grain of the crepe paper runs from the top of the petal to the bottom. Place the template on top of the pile, draw around it and cut out the petals.

3. Holding both sides of the pile of petals between your thumbs and index fingers, gently pull them apart to make the petals curl.

4. Cut a disk of white crepe paper 3/4" in diameter and place it in the bottom of one of the compartments in the cupcake pan. Fix three of the petals to the disk with white craft glue. The petals should overlap.

CONT. >>>

5. Glue the remaining petals on top of the first three so they all overlap. Finish with a blob of glue ready for the next step.

6. Use pinking shears to cut a disk of black crepe paper 3¼" in diameter. Make ¾" snips all around the disk to create the stamens. Glue this in the center of the white petals.

7. Roll some scraps of black crepe paper into a ball about ¾" in diameter. Cover this with a piece of black crepe paper and smooth it into a pebble shape. Glue it in the center of the anemone and leave to dry.

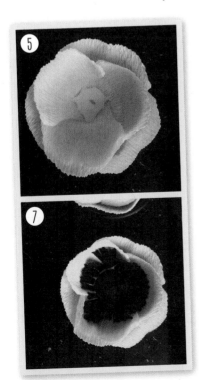

TO MAKE THE CAMELLIAS

8. Copy the camellia petal templates on page 120 onto thin cardboard.

9. Using the templates, cut four small, seven medium, and five large petals from white crepe paper.

10. Stretch and curl the petals as before.

11. Cut another disk of white crepe roughly 1¼" in diameter and place it in the bottom of a cupcake compartment. Glue the five large petals onto the disk so they overlap each other slightly.

12. Glue the seven medium petals onto the large ones, again making sure they all overlap. It's best to do this in two stages: first making a round of four petals, then a round of three.

13. Glue the four small petals in place on top. To make the center of the camellia, cut a rectangle of white crepe 1¼" x 6" and fold it widthwise into fifths. Cut a deep arch along one of the short edges of the folded rectangle so when you open it out, you have a scalloped edge.

14. Roll the scalloped rectangle into a flower bud shape and glue to the center of the flower. Leave to dry.

TO MAKE THE BUDS, SMALLER FLOWERS, AND LEAVES

15. To make a bud, cover a ³⁄₄" paper or polystyrene ball in a piece of white crepe paper. Glue it in place underneath the ball.

16. Cut a 1¼" x 9½" rectangle of white crepe paper and fold it into eighths. The grain should run sideways.

17. Cut a deep arch along one of the short edges of the folded paper, as before.

18. Open out the scalloped rectangle and fix one end underneath the ball. Gently stretch and wrap the rectangle around the ball, gluing it in place as you go. Leave to dry.

19. To make the smaller flowers, cut scalloped rectangles and roll them up in the same way as you made the camellia centers.

20. Use pinking shears to cut leaf shapes from the lime green crepe paper.

TO MAKE THE BOUQUET

21. Make approximately 16 anemones, 12 camellias, eight buds, and some leaves.

22. Cover the 6" polystyrene ball in white crepe paper and place it in a small bowl or mug so it doesn't roll around.

23. Start pinning the larger flowers into the ball: a couple of pins in each flower should hold it in place. When you are happy with the arrangement, glue the flowers in place more securely. Use the buds and make leaves and smaller flowers to fill any gaps between the large flowers.

24. Fold the ribbon in half and glue and pin it in place at the top of the bouquet so it can hang from the bride's wrist.

EXTRA!

If possible, buy good-quality florist's crepe paper. It has amazing stretch and durability that cheaper papers don't possess.

FLORAL GIFT BOX GARLAND

The uses for these delicate little flowers are endless. Here, they are the finishing touches to a beautifully wrapped gift, but they could also be used on a greeting card or as place settings. A collection of flowers in the middle of a table would be nice and the teeny tiny ones would be beautiful as confetti.

SUPPLIES

Two 3¼" squares of colored paper, for large flowers

Two 2" squares of colored paper, for small flowers

1½" squares of colored paper, for leaves

Scissors

Craft knife and cutting mat

Metal ruler

Bradawl

Small metal cotter pins

Length of thin ribbon or gold cord (optional)

Gift box

Glue stick or glue dots

makes 1

TO MAKE THE FLOWERS

1. Using the templates on page 120, trace and cut the petals shapes from colored paper. You need two petals shapes in different colors for each finished flower.

2. Take one of the petals shapes and, using the blunt back edge of the craft knife, score two straight lines as marked on the template (A and B). Turn the shape over and score the two diagonal lines marked in blue (C and D).

3. Fold the petals shape along the line marked A. Open it out and fold again along the line marked B, then turn it over and fold along the lines marked C and D.

CONT. 〉〉〉

4. Working around the shape, pinch each quarter together to give a slightly three-dimensional effect.

5. Repeat steps 1–4 with another piece of paper in a different color.

6. Using a bradawl and resting the paper on a piece of wood, make a hole in the center of each petals shape.

7. Place one petals shape on top of another and push a cotter pin through the two holes. Arrange the petals so both sets are visible.

8. Repeat steps 1–7 until you have made as many flowers as you like.

TO MAKE THE LEAVES

9. Using the template on page 120, trace and cut out the leaves shapes from colored paper. Score a line three-quarters of the way down the center of the leaf and crease.

10. To use the flowers and leaves to decorate a gift box, make holes in the leaves and thread them onto some thin ribbon or gold cord and wrap around the box. Use a small amount of glue or a glue dot to fix the flowers in place on the top of the box.

ROSE GIFT TAG

These roses are possibly the simplest but most effective paper flowers there are. They can be made tiny or giant, but are beautiful, whatever their size.

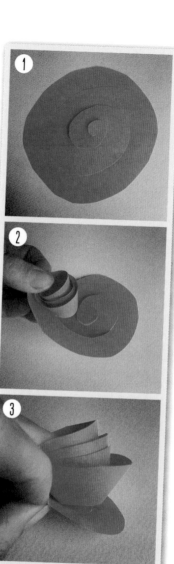

EXTRA!

These roses look really cute glued to branches of twisted willow for a springtime table centerpiece.

1. Cut a spiral from a square of paper. Make sure the spiral is neither too wide nor too narrow. If you prefer, you can draw the spiral onto the paper before cutting.

2. Starting at the outside edge, roll the spiral up, holding it firmly to stop it from unrolling.

3. When you get to the end of the spiral, use a nice blob of glue from a glue gun on the center to hold the rose petals in place.

4. Make clusters of roses in different sizes and in a variety of colors to decorate your gifts. Additionally, make a few leaves to accompany the roses following the instructions on page 53.

PASSION FLOWER GIFT TAG

Passion flowers are one of my favorite flowers. Although this is a stylized version of a passion flower, designed to be used as a gift tag, it is just as gorgeous as the real thing.

SUPPLIES

Thin cardboard, for templates

Pencil

Scissors

Metal ruler

Craft knife and cutting mat

5½" square of purple paper

2¾" square of white paper

¾" x 5" rectangle of yellow paper

Clear tape

makes 1

1. Copy the enlarged templates on page 120 onto thin cardboard and use them to cut out the large flower shape from the purple paper and the small flower shape from the white paper.

2. On one side of the flowers, score along the dotted lines as shown on the template, then flip the flowers over and score along the dashed lines.

3. Work around the flowers, concertinaing the petals as you go. The flowers will begin to close in on themselves. Cut a small hole in the center of each flower.

4. Roll the rectangle of yellow paper around a pencil, fixing it at one end with a short piece of clear tape.

5. Remove the pencil and cut the rectangle into several thin strips along its length until you reach the tape. Curl each strip with scissors to make the curly center of the passion flower.

6. Insert the curly center into the white flower, then put both inside the purple flower. The tape at the end will act as a stopper.

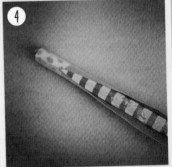

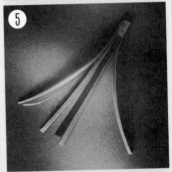

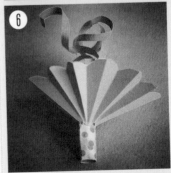

With Love
Christine xxx

DAISY GIFT TAG

This clever little flower holds a surprise inside. Open it up and the bloom reveals a hidden message at its center.

SUPPLIES

Thin cardboard, for templates

8" square of yellow paper

4" square of orange paper

3¼" square of white paper

2½" x 4" rectangle of green paper

White craft glue

Scissors

Craft knife and cutting mat

Metal ruler

makes 1

1. Copy the enlarged templates on page 120 onto thin cardboard and use them to cut out one yellow daisy, one orange base flower, and three green leaves. Gently score along the lines on the daisy shape where indicated.

2. Starting at the top and working all the way around the daisy, fold the petals inward along the five diagonal scored lines.

3. Pinch each petal together along the six straight scored lines.

4. Starting at one side and working in a clockwise direction, gently press the petals down. They will fall to the side and overlap each other to close up the flower. This may require a little wiggling and gentle persuasion!

5. Open up the flower again and glue the daisy center in place. Write a message on it, if you so wish. Glue the daisy to the orange base flower.

6. Score and crease each leaf approximately half way along their spines. Glue the leaves between the yellow daisy and the orange base flower.

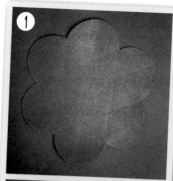

OWL GIFT BOXES

Fill these cute little boxes with candies to make great goodie bags for parties. Or they are the perfect size for the safe delivery of baubles, bangles, and beads.

TO MAKE THE BOX

1. Using the enlarged template from page 121, trace the owl gift box onto the piece of thin cardboard.

2. Place the cardboard on the cutting mat and stick the edges down with masking tape so it will not move around when you are cutting.

3. Using the craft knife, cut out the owl's face where marked on the template: cut away his eyes, eyebrows, and wings, but only make slits for his beak and tummy feathers.

4. Cut out the rest of the owl, except the teeth on the side flaps—it is easier to do this later.

5. Score where shown on the template—the curve at the top of the owl's head, the curve at the top of his back, the four lines around the base of the box, the four lines along the edges of the side flaps, and the lines for the beak and feathers where indicated.

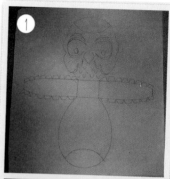

CONT. >>>

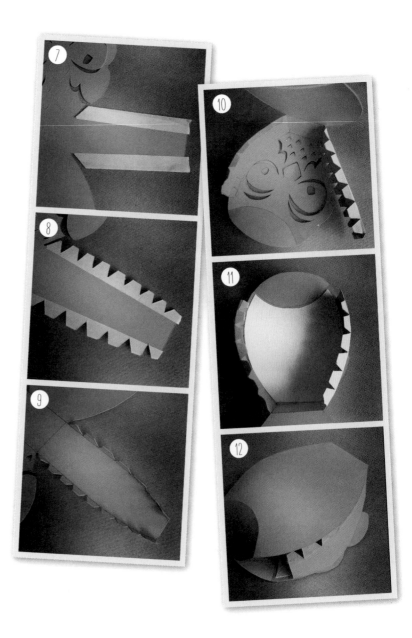

〉〉〉

6. Using the enlarged template on page 121, cut out the insert from the 6" square of cardboard.

7. Fix strips of double-sided tape along both edges of the side flaps. Cut the tape in line with the scored lines as shown so no tape is visible once the box is made up.

8. Cut notches in the edges of the flaps to create "teeth." These help the flaps bend in a smooth curve, following the shape of the owl.

9. Fold the flaps up along the scored lines and remove the protective backing from the tape.

10. Lay the owl face down on a clean, flat surface and fold up the base and sides to start forming the box. Press one side flap onto the owl, following his shape. Repeat on the other side.

11. Place a short strip of double-sided tape on the inside of the box behind the owl's face and attach the insert.

12. Fold up the owl's back onto the other edge of the flaps. Press to fix in place.

13. Fold closed the curved flap at the top of his head and the curved flap at the top of his back and fix in place with a piece of washi tape. Your owl is born!

GIANT HAREBELL STRING OF LIGHTS

The whiteness of the lightbulbs in a string of LED lights creates a beautiful glow inside these pretty harebell shapes. Try white paper for snowdrops or yellow paper for cowslips.

SAFETY NOTE
Although LED lights do not give out much heat, never leave them on overnight or unattended.

TO MAKE THE FLOWERS

1. Make a thin cardboard template from the shape on page 121. Trim a sheet of colored paper to a 8¼" square.

2. Fold the paper square into quarters (run a ruler or your fingernails along each crease to make the creases really sharp). Place the folded paper on a clean, flat surface as a diamond shape, with the unfolded edges of the paper at the bottom.

3. Fold the right-hand side of the diamond into the center. Repeat with the left-hand side to form a kite shape.

4. Open out the folds to make a diamond shape again. Place the template on the folded paper as shown and trace around it.

CONT. >>>

5. Using scissors, cut away the excess paper from the diamond shape.

6. Open the flower halfway and re-crease the small V-shaped fold at the top of each petal so it is sharp and will easily fold both ways.

7. Open out the flower and fold the V-shaped creases inward to create valley folds (see pages 12–13 for an explanation of a valley fold).

8. Using a glue stick, spread glue over the valley folds of one petal and press it to the two petals on either side of it to make the flower shape. Repeat to join all four petals.

9. Your flat piece of paper should now be a bell shape.

10. Using scissors, curl the base of each petal upward to form a flower-shaped paper shade.

11. Make as many paper flowers as there are lightbulbs in your string of fairy lights. Snip a small hole in the top of each paper shade and gently push each one onto a lightbulb.

FOLK ART WALL STARS

TOP TIP

As some wallpapers are quite fibrous, they can stretch and bend more than thinner papers. This makes wallpaper better suited to the three-dimensionality of this project. Other types of paper may tear when you bend the star.

These paper stars are reminiscent of the wooden good-luck symbols found in folk art. Using large sheets of card and offcuts of wallpaper means you can make the stars as big as you like.

SUPPLIES

Pencil

Metal ruler

3 mm-thick gray cardboard

Craft knife and cutting mat

Scraps of wallpaper or other medium-weight paper

Spray adhesive

Double-sided tape

Hole punch or bradawl

Length of string or ribbon for hanging

Scissors

makes 1

TO MAKE THE STAR

1. Using the enlarged template on page 122 at your preferred size, trace the star outline onto the thick cardboard. Using a pencil and ruler, draw the lines between the star points where indicated on the template.

2. Using a metal ruler and craft knife, cut out the star from the cardboard. Turn the star over and draw pencil lines between the points of the star as before.

3. On one side of the star, score the five short lines marked in red on the template.

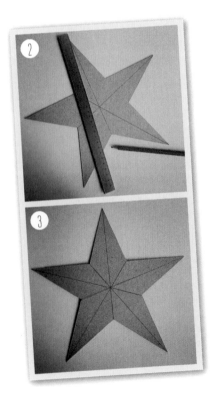

CONT. >>>

This Folk Art Star Garland is made from patterned paper, rather than covered cardboard. Using the same template and method as the Folk Art Wall Stars, make a selection of paper stars in three different sizes—6", 4³/₄", and 3¹/₂" from point to point—scoring the lines on the reverse only. Arrange the paper stars in a pleasing order and then pass a needle threaded with a length of cotton embroidery thread through one point of each star to cluster them together.

4. Turn the star over and score the five long lines marked in blue on the template.

5. With this side facing upward, gently pinch and manipulate each star point until they become three-dimensional.

TO COVER THE STAR

6. Lay a piece of wallpaper right side down on a clean, flat surface. Spray the front of the star with spray adhesive, then place it on the wallpaper. Press the star flat. Cut around it, leaving a 3/4" margin of wallpaper all the way around.

7. At each inner point of the star, trim away some of the wallpaper as shown. Place a strip of double-sided tape along each side of each star point. Remove its protective backing.

8. Fold the edges of the wallpaper back onto the double-sided tape, trimming away any excess at the tip of the star points.

9. Turn the star over and gently reshape it. Using a hole punch or bradawl, make a hole in the top of one of the star points and thread a length of string or ribbon through to make a hanging loop.

WATERLILY TABLE CENTERPIECE

Thin cardboard, for templates

17" x 22" pieces of white (or cream) slightly translucent or patterned medium-weight paper

Yellow translucent paper or tissue paper

Scissors

Craft knife and cutting mat

Metal ruler

Pencil

Glue stick

LED night lights

22" x 34" piece of green heavyweight paper, for the leaf

makes 1

SAFETY NOTE:
Only use battery-operated LED night lights; never use a candle with a real flame.

Turn your dining table into a tranquil oasis by adding a selection of these light-up waterlilies. The LED night lights will flicker and cast beautiful shadows through the paper and luckily won't set fire to them!

TO MAKE THE FLOWERS

1. Trace and cut the enlarged templates on page 121 from thin cardboard.

2. For the waterlily flowers, either trace around the templates onto the white or cream paper and cut out using scissors, or place the templates on the white paper and cut out using a craft knife. Cut out two large petals and two small petals per flowers.

CONT. >>>

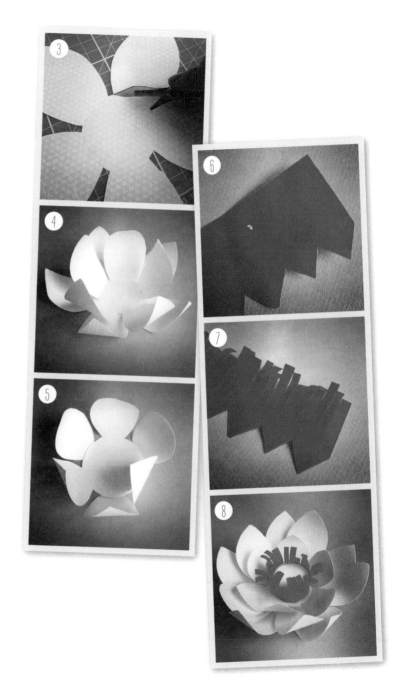

3. Using the blunt back edge of the knife, score each petal of one large flower as indicated by the dotted line on the template. Fold up each petal. Repeat with all the flowers.

4. Place one of the large flowers on top of the other so the petals alternate. Glue in place.

5. Repeat with the small flowers, then glue the pair of small flowers in the center of the large flower, again so the petals alternate.

6. Cut a 2" x 5½" rectangle from the yellow paper. Score a line ⅝" from one long edge and cut rough points along it, spaced approximately ¾" apart.

7. Snip straight cuts about 1" deep and ¼" apart along the other long edge to make the stamens. Curl some of the stamens with the blade of the scissors (see page 13).

8. Roll from the short side of the rectangle to make a tube and join together with a little glue. Fold the rough points inward, glue the underside of these, and use them to fix the stamens to the center of the waterlily. Finally place the LED night light in the center.

TO MAKE THE BUD AND LEAVES

9. A bud is made by gluing the petals shut after a switched-on night light has been placed inside.

10. For the leaves, draw around a dinner plate onto the green heavyweight paper and cut out. Cut away a V-shape with rounded corners at one side of the circle—like a slice of cake.

PAPER GARLANDS

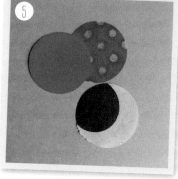

2" circle punch

Selection of medium-weight colored and patterned papers

Sewing machine

Matching sewing thread

Scissors

Needle

Thin cream string (or crochet thread)

Metal ruler

Craft knife and cutting mat

Glue stick

2" flower-shaped punch

makes 1 of each

EXTRA

For a different look, make a garland of spheres close to one another. Don't separate the paper stacks after step 4. Instead, just open them out to make them three-dimensional.

TO MAKE THE SPHERES GARLAND

1. Using the circle punch, cut out 30 disks from the colored paper. If you are using handmade or textured paper, the punch may get stuck. Instead of punching the paper slowly as you would do normally, use a swift whack of the punch. It works much better!

2. Neatly stack three disks of different paper on top of each other. Repeat with all the disks.

3. Place one stack of disks centrally under the foot of your sewing machine. Slowly sew down the center of the stack with long straight stitches.

4. When you reach the edge of the first stack of disks, stop the sewing machine and place another stack under the foot. Repeat until all the stacks are sewn together in a row.

5. Use scissors to separate the stacks. Take the top disk of one stack and fold its two edges toward each other to make it three dimensional. Repeat with the bottom disk. Repeat with all the stacks.

6. Using a needle with string, thread the top of each sphere onto the string so the spheres are equally spaced. Display them somewhere lovely.

TO MAKE THE FLAG GARLAND

1. Using a metal ruler and craft knife, cut 1"-wide strips the length of your sheets of paper.

2. Starting at one end of a strip, use scissors to cut two diagonal lines that meet at a point. Repeat this approximately 2½" farther along the strip—it doesn't matter if the flags are different lengths. Repeat until you reach the end of the strip.

3. Using the blunt back edge of the craft knife and a ruler, score a line approximately ¾" down from the flag's point. Fold along the scored line, then unfold.

4. Place the flags on a clean, flat surface so they are equidistant from one another. Arrange them in a pleasing order.

5. Using a glue stick, smear a line of glue along the crease in each flag.

6. Leaving an 8" tail end at both ends, lay a length of string through the middle of the row of flags. Fold the point of each flag over the string, lining them up neatly and securing them in place.

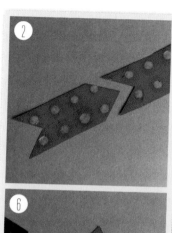
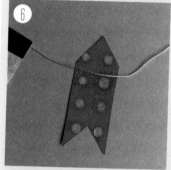
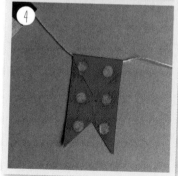

TO MAKE THE FLOWER GARLAND

1. Using the flower punch, cut out 50 flower shapes from the colored paper.

2. Set half of the flowers aside. Place the other half on a clean, flat surface. Arrange the flowers so they are equidistant from one another and the colors and patterns are nicely mixed up.

3. Using a glue stick, place a spot of glue in the center of each flower.

4. Leaving an 8" tail end at both ends, lay a length of string through the middle of the row of flowers. Place a second flower from the half you set aside on top, lining the two up neatly and gluing them together. You can either match the pairs of flowers or vary the colors and patterns on each side of the garland. Repeat with all the flowers.

SHADOW TREE PICTURE

A box frame is perfect for these delicate paper-cut trees and their pretty shadows. The background is effective whether you choose a plain contrasting color, a pattern, or simply go for white on white.

SUPPLIES

8" square of medium-weight watercolor paper

8" square box frame

Pencil

Metal ruler

Thin white paper

Masking tape

Craft knife and cutting mat

Hole punch

Scraps of colored paper

Glue stick

Scissors

makes 1

TO MAKE THE TREE PICTURE

1. Mark a 6¼" square in the center of the watercolor paper— this is the area that will be visible inside the frame. As box frames can vary, you may need to calculate the size of square that works for your particular frame. Instead of drawing lines to indicate the square, only make small pencil marks at each corner; that way there is less chance of the pencil marks being seen once the picture has been framed—which is more likely if the frame isn't quite square.

2. Trace and cut out the template on page 122 from thin white paper. Place it face up in the center of your drawn square and use masking tape to attach it to the watercolor paper.

CONT. >>>

3. Using a craft knife with a sharp blade, cut the tree shapes through the template and the watercolor paper. (Remember the solid line is where you cut; the dotted lines are for scoring and folding, which will be done later.) Cut slowly and carefully, especially when making the V-shaped cuts in the pine tree and the semi-circular cuts in the round bush. Use a ruler for super-straight tree trunks.

4. When all the trees have been cut, remove the template and carefully check your work. Re-cut any areas where your knife blade hasn't quite made it through both layers of paper, usually around the tips of the leaves. Use a hole punch to make a circular hole in the round tree.

5. Use a ruler and the back edge of your craft knife to score the trees along the dotted lines, then gently fold the cut halves of the trees back. Where the cut paper is very narrow, use your knife blade like a shovel to help you turn and fold it.

6. Cut rectangles from the colored-paper scraps, each rectangle just large enough for one tree. Use a glue stick to glue around the edge of each tree and carefully stick one piece of paper behind each tree. Make sure the colored papers do not overlap much or the overlap will be seen behind the finished tree.

7. Turn the picture over and trim away the excess paper so the picture will fit into the box frame.

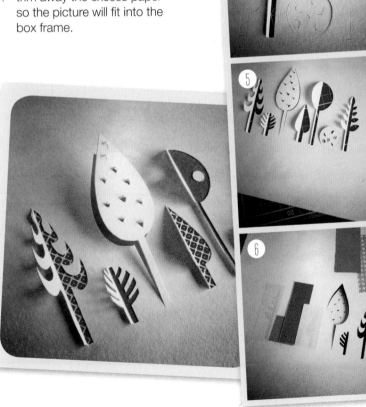

LIFESIZE CARDBOARD DEER

Momma Deer and Baby Deer make quick and effective decorations for winter festivities, but they're also fun to have around any time of the year. Make them any size. The only limit is the size of your cardboard boxes. Both are made the same way.

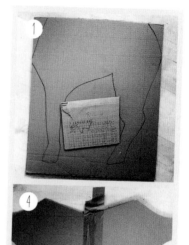

SUPPLIES

Large cardboard boxes

Pencil

Felt-tip pen

Metal ruler

Craft knife or scissors

Parcel or duct tape

Wide double-sided tape

makes 1 of each

TO MAKE THE DEER

1. These lifesize Momma Deer and Baby Deer each need two pieces of cardboard for their body and two for their head. Starting with the body, use a grid to enlarge the deer templates on page 114 and trace onto one piece of the cardboard box. On the grid shown, the scale is $3/8$" equals $2\,3/4$".

2. Cut out the cardboard using a craft knife or scissors. If using a craft knife, rest the cardboard on a suitable surface.

3. Place the cut-out body on top of the other piece of cardboard, draw around it and cut out the second body section.

4. Lay both sections on a flat surface so the upper edges are touching and the gridded sides are face up. Use lengths of parcel or duct tape to tape them together. This is the deer's spine. Trim away any excess tape.

5. Repeat steps 1–3 to make the two sections of the deer's head. Place both sections on a flat surface and tape them together along the top of the neck.

6. Attach strips of double-sided tape to the body where indicated on the template and fix the head to the body.

7. Enlarge and cut out the tail. Fold it in half where indicated and attach it to the deer's bottom with double-sided tape.

FEATHER MOBILE

I love all the bright colors in these mobiles and the way the feathers move in the breeze. It's also a great way to use up all your scraps of paper.

SUPPLIES

Pencil

Thin cardboard, for templates

Spray adhesive

Selection of scraps of paper in various colors and patterns

Paper clip

Scissors

Needle

Selection of colored cotton threads

5½" diameter wooden embroidery hoop

Tape measure

⅝"-wide washi tape or colored masking tape

Strong sewing thread or embroidery thread, for hanging

makes 1

TO MAKE THE FEATHERS

1. Using the templates on pages 122–123, trace the four feather outlines onto thin cardboard.

2. Spray the wrong side of one sheet of colored paper with adhesive and glue it to a second sheet of colored paper so that you have a double-sided sheet. Repeat with several sheets of paper so you have a mix and match of colors and patterns on each side.

3. Place a feather template on top of two or three pieces of double-sided paper and clip them together with a paper clip. Using scissors, cut out the feather shapes from the double-sided paper.

CONT. >>>

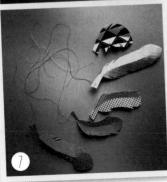

4. Repeat step 3 using the other templates until you have approximately 30 feathers.

5. Snip away little pieces of paper from the edge of the feathers for a real feather-like effect.

6. Score down the center of each feather with the scissors, as shown on the templates and crease the feathers along the scored lines.

TO HANG THE FEATHERS

7. Using a needle, thread the end of each feather onto a length of cotton thread. Vary the lengths of thread so they measure between 2" and 8".

8. Measure the circumference of the outside of the embroidery hoop. Cut a piece of washi tape or colored masking tape to this length and lay it on a flat surface, sticky side up. Lay the lengths of cotton with their feathers along the tape so some feathers hang lower than others.

9. Roll the embroidery hoop along the tape from one end to the other. The hoop will pick up the tape and feathers as it goes.

10. Trim away any excess cotton and fold the excess washi tape over to the inside of the hoop.

11. To hang the mobile, cut two 20" lengths of strong sewing or embroidery thread. Tie one end of one length to the hoop and the other end to the opposite side of the hoop. Repeat, attaching the second length of thread to the other two quarter points of the hoop.

RUSTIC QUILLED DECORATIONS

Quilling is the art of rolling thin strips of paper into a variety of coils and shapes to make small intricate patterns. Using corrugated cardboard means you can supersize the quilled decorations, which are perfect for autumnal or winter festivities.

CONT. >>>

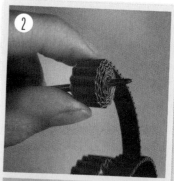

SUPPLIES

Roll of brown corrugated cardboard

Scissors

Ruler

Cookie cutters in heart shapes and other chosen shapes

Thin knitting needle

Glue dots

White craft glue

Ribbon, for hanging

Hair dryer

makes 1 heart and 1 snowflake

TO MAKE THE HEART SHAPE

1. Cut several ³⁄₈"-wide strips from the corrugated cardboard. Cut these strips into various lengths; the length of the strip determines the size of the coil—the longer the strip, the larger the coil.

2. Place a heart-shaped cookie cutter on a clean, flat surface. Holding the knitting needle in one hand, start winding a cardboard strip tightly around the needle to create a coil.

3. Once the coil is the desired size, use a glue dot to fix the free end of the strip to the coil. Slip the coil off the knitting needle and place it inside the cookie cutter. To make a coil with a more open center, slip it from the knitting needle before gluing the free end in place, let the coil unravel slightly, then glue the end.

4. Make several different-size coils and place them inside the cookie cutter so it starts to fill up.

5. Once the cookie cutter is full of larger coils, start making smaller ones to fit into the gaps. Continue until the cookie cutter is completely filled.

6. Turn the cookie cutter over (the coils should be firmly held in place so they should not fall out) and place it back on your surface. Pat the coils down so they are level on the underside.

7. Cover the top of the coils with white craft glue (7A), spreading it evenly so it covers all the coils (7B). Try not to get glue on the cookie cutter as makes it harder to get the finished decoration out later. Leave to dry overnight.

8. Once completely dry, remove the decoration from the cutter. Use a craft knife to loosen any glue holding the coils to the cutter. If any coils fall out, simply glue them back in place.

9. Thread a length of ribbon through one of the open coils to hang the decoration.

TO MAKE THE SNOWFLAKE

These snowflake decorations do not rely on a cookie cutter to create the shape. Once you learn the basic shapes, you can create any pattern you like.

1. Cut seven $3/4$" x $27^1/2$" strips from corrugated cardboard.

2. Roll one strip into a tight, round coil to form the center of the snowflake. This coil should be approximately $1^1/4$" in diameter.

3. Make a crease in another strip, 8" from one end. Roll a tight coil into this crease, then fix in place using a glue dot. Roll the rest of the strip into a relaxed coil around it.

4. Hold the coil tightly in one hand (between thumb and index finger is easiest) and squash it into an oval shape approximately $2^1/4$" long (this may require a little adjustment of the relaxed coil to get the right size). Fix the free end in place with a glue dot.

5. Pinch the relaxed coil between your thumb and index finger to create a teardrop shape.

6. Coat one side of the rounded half of the teardrop with white craft glue and hold it in place until it is tacky (a hair dryer helps speed this up). To make the other points of the snowflake, repeat steps 3–6.

7. Cut one of your $3/4$" x $27^{1}/_{2}$" strips into five 4" lengths and roll these into tight coils. On a flat surface arrange the coils and teardrops into a snowflake shape.

8. Cover the snowflake with white craft glue, making sure you spread it over all areas where the coils and teardrops meet. Leave to dry overnight.

9. Once completely dry, thread a length of ribbon through the top point of the snowflake to hang or simply stand.

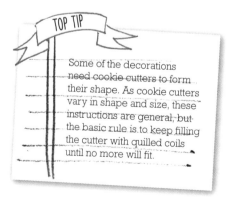

TOP TIP

Some of the decorations need cookie cutters to form their shape. As cookie cutters vary in shape and size, these instructions are general, but the basic rule is to keep filling the cutter with quilled coils until no more will fit.

SHIMMERING FISHES MOBILE

The variety of papers used to make the fish in this mobile all catch the light in different ways making it almost as mesmerizing as if you were snorkeling alongside them. Coloring the watercolor paper with ink gives an added watery feel.

Selection of medium-weight papers—translucent, patterned, plain, and watercolor

Hole punch

Circle cutter or 2" circle punch

Large dinner plate

Medium-size paintbrush

Dark blue and turquoise ink

Roll of paper towels

Sewing machine

Pale blue thread

makes 1

TO MAKE THE FISH

1. Using the templates on page 123, cut 17 fish from the different papers.

2. Use a hole punch to make an eye in each of the paper fish. Don't worry about precise eye positions—it's better if the fish aren't all identical.

3. Fill a large dinner plate with cold water. Submerge each of the watercolor-paper fish in the water and leave to soak for 10 seconds.

CONT. >>>

4. Remove the fish from the water and place on a sheet of paper towel. Using the paintbrush dipped in ink, make a line along the belly edge of the fish; the ink will bleed up the paper to create a watery pattern. Leave to dry. If the paper fish has gone a bit wobbly from the water, once dry, press flat with a cool iron.

TO MAKE THE SPHERE

5. Using the circle cutter, cut three disks of paper.

TO CONSTRUCT THE MOBILE

6. Lay the fish out on a clean, flat surface and arrange them until you are happy with the order. Place some fish facing to the left and others facing to the right.

7. You are now going to machine-stitch all the fish together to form a long string. Leave a 12" length of thread pulled through the sewing machine needle before stitching. This is for hanging the mobile. Place your first fish under the foot of the sewing machine so the needle is roughly in the center of its spine. Sew slowly with long straight stitches. Just as you are coming to the belly edge of the first fish, stop the sewing machine, raise the foot and place the next fish so it butts up to the first. Lower the foot and continue sewing.

8. Repeat until you have stitched the last fish, then place the three disks of the sphere on top of each other, butting them up to the last fish. Stitch through the center of the disks. Fan out the disks to make the sphere.

9. Using the 12" thread, hang the mobile in a gentle breeze.

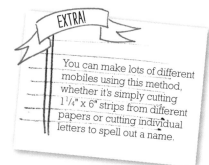

EXTRA!

You can make lots of different mobiles using this method, whether it's simply cutting 1¼" x 6" strips from different papers or cutting individual letters to spell out a name.

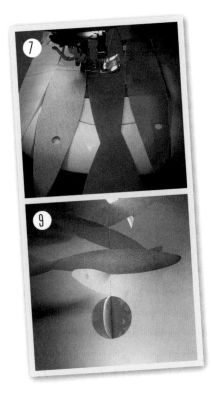

ROCOCO MIRROR FRAME

It's hard to believe that this mirror frame is made from plain old brown packaging paper. Its crisp lines and elegant curves belie its humble origins.

TO MAKE THE FRAME

1. Place the mirror you are making a frame for on the mounting board and draw around it.

2. Measure and mark $3/8$" out and $3/4$" in from your drawn line to mark the cutting lines of the mounting board frame.

3. Using a craft knife and cutting mat, cut away the inside edge of the frame followed by the outside edge.

EXTRA!

The layout of this frame works well for any shape. If you have an old wooden frame that you want to revamp, you could simply decorate it with the paper curlicues and flowers.

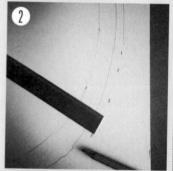

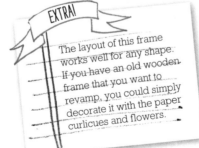

CONT. >>>

4. Cover the board frame with a thin layer of white craft glue. First squeeze it on, then spread it out evenly with a scrap of of cardboard.

5. Lay a piece of brown paper on a flat surface and place the frame, glue side down, on top.

6. Turn the frame over and smooth out any obvious lumps and creases. Little creases will vanish as the glue dries.

TO DECORATE THE FRAME

7. While the frame dries, make the paper flowers and curlicues. Use the flower punches or the daisy template from page 120 to cut five large flowers and ten small ones from the brown paper, corrugated cardboard, and silver and gold papers. Pinch each of the petals together to make the flowers three-dimensional.

8. Stick the brown paper to the thin brown cardboard with spray glue. Using the templates from page 124, cut out one each of curlicues A, B, and C. Flip the templates for curlicues A and B and cut a second set of curlicues that are a mirror image of the first.

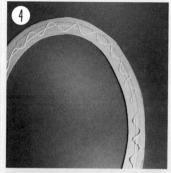

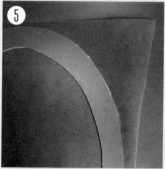

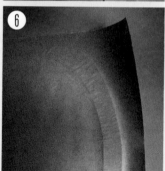

9. Score along the lines shown and carefully pinch the curlicues so they become three-dimensional. It is best to start at a point and work away from it, following each curve.

10. Use the templates to make the leaves. Cut some with pinking shears. Carefully fold each leaf along its spine to make it three-dimensional.

11. Start building up the frame. First trim the excess brown paper from the inside and outside edges of the frame, then place the largest curlicues at the top of the frame and the smaller ones at the bottom. Arrange the flowers and leaves around them. When you are happy with the design, use a glue gun to fix everything in place.

12. Scrunch up little pieces of paper to make the centers of flowers and attach them with the glue gun.

13. Use the glue gun to attach the cardboard frame to the mirror.

GIANT GIFT ROSETTES

Selection of lengths of wallpaper (see below)

Craft knife

Metal ruler

Cutting mat

Stapler

Double-sided tape

Ribbon or string

Strong clear tape

Using a craft knife, metal ruler, and cutting mat, cut strips of wallpaper into the following lengths to make large, medium and small bows.

For a large rosette (20" in diameter)

One 4" x 16" strip

Two 4$\frac{1}{4}$" x 36" strips

Four 4$\frac{1}{4}$" x 40" strips

For a medium rosette (16" in diameter)

One 3$\frac{1}{4}$" x 8" strip

Two 3$\frac{1}{2}$" x 27$\frac{1}{2}$" strips

Four 3$\frac{1}{2}$" x 31$\frac{1}{2}$" strips

For a small rosette (24cm diameter)

One 2" x 6" strip

Two 2$\frac{1}{4}$" x 16" strips

Four 2$\frac{1}{4}$" x 20" strips

makes 3 rosettes of different sizes

A cluster of these supersized rosettes—usually made from shiny plasticized ribbon and used for decorating presents—makes an impressive wall display in your home or for a party. They are a great way of using up spare lengths of wallpaper.

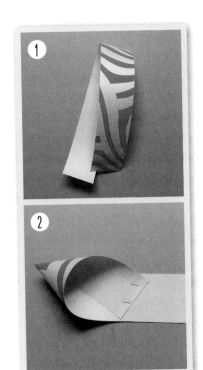

TO MAKE EACH ROSETTE

1. Fold one of the longest strips of wallpaper in half to find the center.

2. Twist one end of the wallpaper strip so it meets the center fold. Staple in place.

CONT. >>>

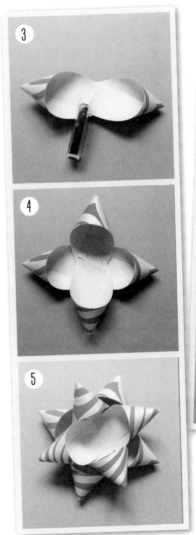

3. Repeat with the other end of the wallpaper strip.

4. Repeat steps 1–3 with another of the longest strips. Put two pieces of double-sided tape on the bottom of this second strip and fix it inside the first so the two are at right angles to each other. This makes the first layer of the rosette.

5. Repeat steps 1–3 with the other two longest strips, placing each one inside the first layer of the rosette and fixing them with double-sided tape as in step 4.

6. Repeat steps 1–4 with the two shorter strips and place these inside the rosette.

7. Roll the short strip of paper loosely and staple the ends together. Place some double-sided tape on the bottom and fix it in the center of the rosette.

8. Attach a length of ribbon or string to the back of each rosette using strong clear tape. Your rosette is now ready to hang on the wall.

BOW GARLAND

I love this bow garland. It turns normal boring stationery supplies into something beautiful. (Though if the truth be told, I never find stationery supplies boring!)

SUPPLIES

Brown packaging paper

Craft knife and cutting mat

Metal ruler

White, purple, and neon yellow round stickers

White ring reinforcers

Pencil

Paper clips

Scissors

Glue sheet or double-sided tape

Glue dots

Needle

1¼ yd of butcher's string or embroidery thread in your chosen color

makes 1

TO MAKE THE BOWS

1. For a garland approximately 95" long, cut out thirty 8" x 8¾" rectangles of brown paper. Decorate each with randomly placed colored stickers and white ring reinforcers.

2. Fold one brown paper rectangle in half widthwise and, using the template on page 123, trace the bow outline onto the paper with the center of the bow is against the fold line.

3. Fold the remaining rectangles in half, as before. Stack three together, with the folds on the same side. Place the folded rectangle with the bow drawn on top, then paper clip all the sheets together to secure. Cut out the bow through all layers using scissors. It may be easier to use a craft knife to cut out the middle of the loops.

CONT. >>>

4. Remove the paper clips and open out the bows. Repeat with the rest of the rectangles.

5. With one of the bows patterned side up, place a piece of glue sheet or a narrow strip of double-sided tape down its center over the fold.

6. Place another bow on top, patterned side down. The two bows are now joined in the middle.

7. Repeat with the other bows until you have 15 pairs of bows, all with their patterned sides glued together.

TO CONSTRUCT THE GARLAND

8. Place one pair of bows on a clean, flat surface. Put a glue dot in the middle of both the left and right loops of the bow. Place another pair of bows on top, pressing firmly so the glue dots join the bows together.

9. Repeat, joining all the pairs of bows together. As you go, you will notice that when you lift the top bow up, the rest follow, like a concertina made of bows.

10. When you reach the last pair of bows, use a glue dot to join the left and right loops of the final bow to each other. Then pass the needle and butcher's string or embroidery thread through the center of the glue dot, leaving about 22" for hanging the garland. Repeat at the other end of the garland.

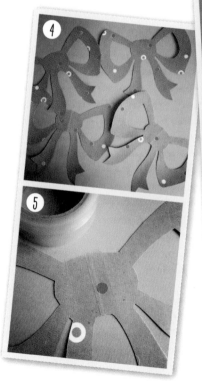

THE AMAZING AERIAL ACROBATS

Watch as Anna, Arabella, and Adèle perform at death-defying heights, swaying in the breeze with their diamonds and pearls glistening in the spotlight.

SUPPLIES

For each acrobat

Pencil

Thin cardboard, for templates

Craft knife and cutting mat

Letter-size sheet of medium-weight, double-sided flesh-colored paper, for the body

Scraps of colored and patterned paper, for the leotard, shoes, and feathers

Glue stick

Self-adhesive jewels

Scissors

Narrow double-sided tape

Pinking shears or other decorative-edged scissors

2¼" × 10¼" rectangle of colored tissue paper

1½" × 10¼" rectangle of tissue paper in a second color

Needle

Silver thread

8" square of double-sided thin gold cardboard, for the moon

makes 1 of each

TO MAKE EACH ACROBAT

1. Copy the templates on page 125 onto thin cardboard. Use a craft knife and cutting mat to cut out all the pieces from the colored papers. If you are using paper that is only patterned on one side for the acrobat's shoes or leotard, make sure the pattern is on the correct side.

TO MAKE THE FLYING GIRLS

2. To make either Anna or Arabella, the flying girls, use a glue stick to stick the leotard, hair, and shoes in place.

3. Add self-adhesive jewels to her wrists, neck, and headpiece. To make the feathers, fold each feather shape in half lengthwise and snip away narrow triangles of paper.

CONT. >>>

4. To make the skirts, place a piece of double-sided tape across the flying girl's waist front, and back, and trim it to the shape of her leotard. Remove the protective backing from the tape.

5. Trim one long edge of the larger rectangle of tissue paper with pinking shears or decorative-edged scissors. Starting at the flying girl's back, gather the tissue paper onto the double-sided tape, pressing it down to fix in place.

6. Repeat steps 4 and 5 with the smaller piece of tissue paper.

7. Glue the flying girl's belt to her skirt to cover up the raw edges.

8. To hang, run a needle threaded with silver thread through the top of the flying girl's head and hang her from a hook or thumbtack in the ceiling.

TO MAKE THE MOON GIRL

9. To make Adèle the moon girl, repeat steps 1–3 then glue Adèle to her moon.

10. To make her train, cut an $3\frac{1}{4}$" length of double-sided tape and place it on the work surface, sticky side up. Cut $2\frac{1}{4}$" off the length of the narrower rectangle of tissue paper, trim with pinking shears or decorative-edged scissors all around and cut one end into a curve. Gather the tissue paper onto the double-sided tape.

11. Trim the wider rectangle of tissue paper so it is the same width as the smaller one. Remove the protective backing from the double-sided tape and gather the top third of this rectangle of tissue paper onto it. Gather the rest of the rectangle and attach it to Adèle's bottom with glue. Glue the heart over the top.

12. Hang by running a needle and thread through the top of the moon.

TEMPLATES

COLORADO CRITTERS

Page 14

These templates are actual size.

——— cut   – – – fold

LIFESIZE
CARDBOARD DEER

Page 84

Referring to this grid, trace the deer body
and head outlines onto cardboard, enlarging
each ³/₈" square to a 2 ³/₄" square.

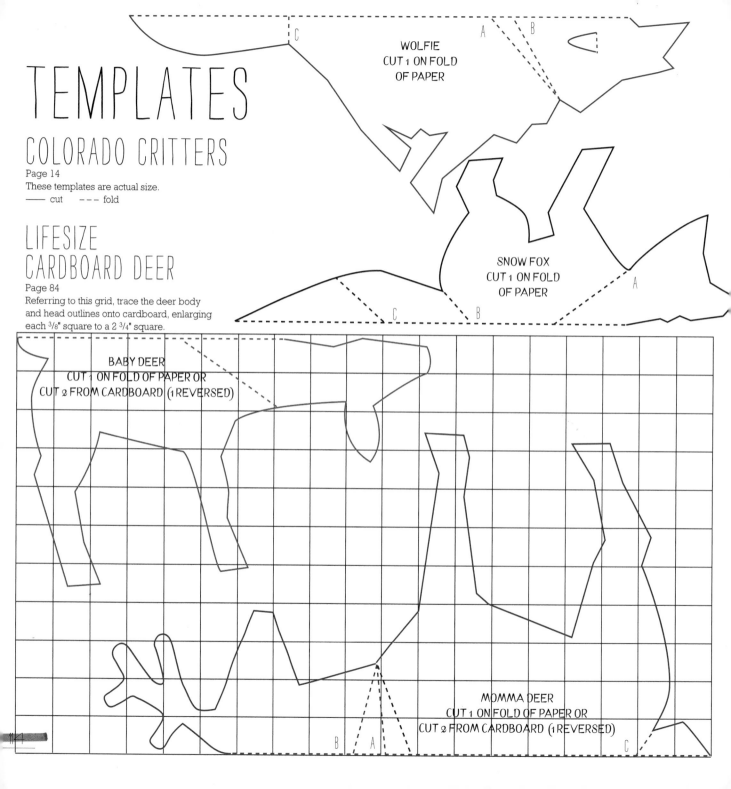

WOLFIE
CUT 1 ON FOLD
OF PAPER

C

A   B

SNOW FOX
CUT 1 ON FOLD
OF PAPER

C   B   A

BABY DEER
CUT 1 ON FOLD OF PAPER OR
CUT 2 FROM CARDBOARD (1 REVERSED)

MOMMA DEER
CUT 1 ON FOLD OF PAPER OR
CUT 2 FROM CARDBOARD (1 REVERSED)

B   A   C

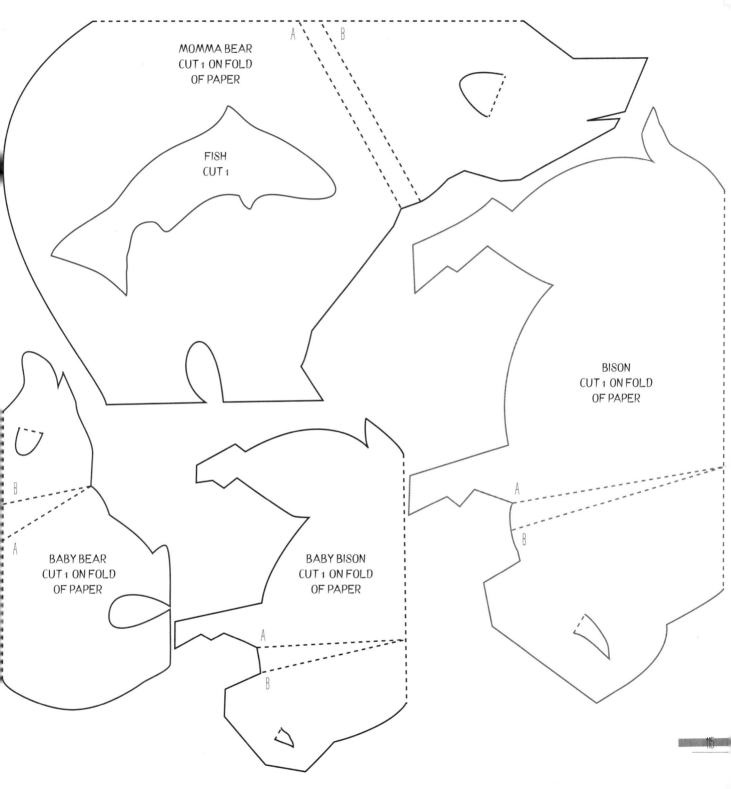

MOMMA BEAR
CUT 1 ON FOLD
OF PAPER

FISH
CUT 1

A

B

BISON
CUT 1 ON FOLD
OF PAPER

A

B

B

A

BABY BEAR
CUT 1 ON FOLD
OF PAPER

BABY BISON
CUT 1 ON FOLD
OF PAPER

A

B

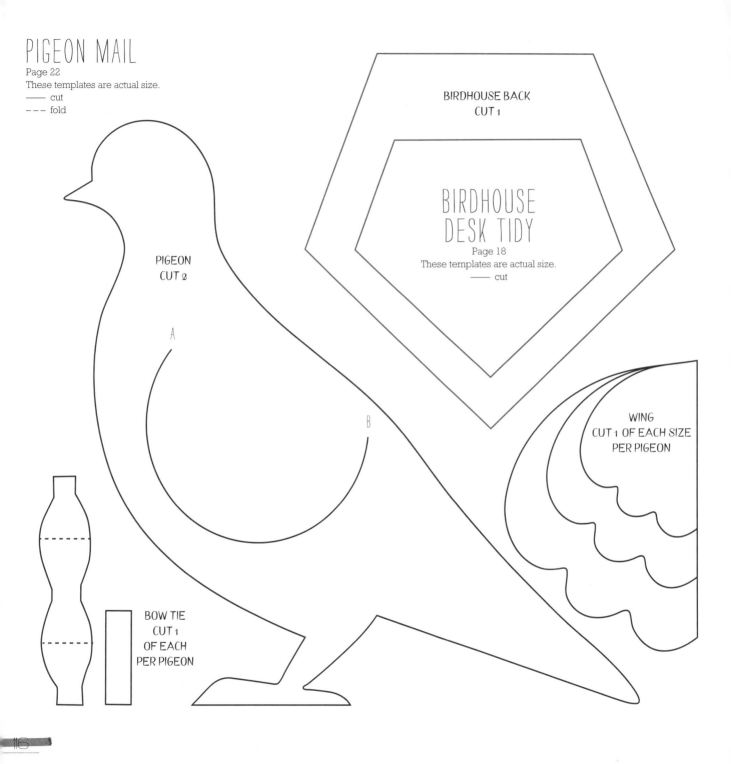

PIGEON MAIL

Page 22
These templates are actual size.
—— cut
– – – fold

PIGEON
CUT 2

A

B

BOW TIE
CUT 1
OF EACH
PER PIGEON

BIRDHOUSE BACK
CUT 1

BIRDHOUSE
DESK TIDY

Page 18
These templates are actual size.
—— cut

WING
CUT 1 OF EACH SIZE
PER PIGEON

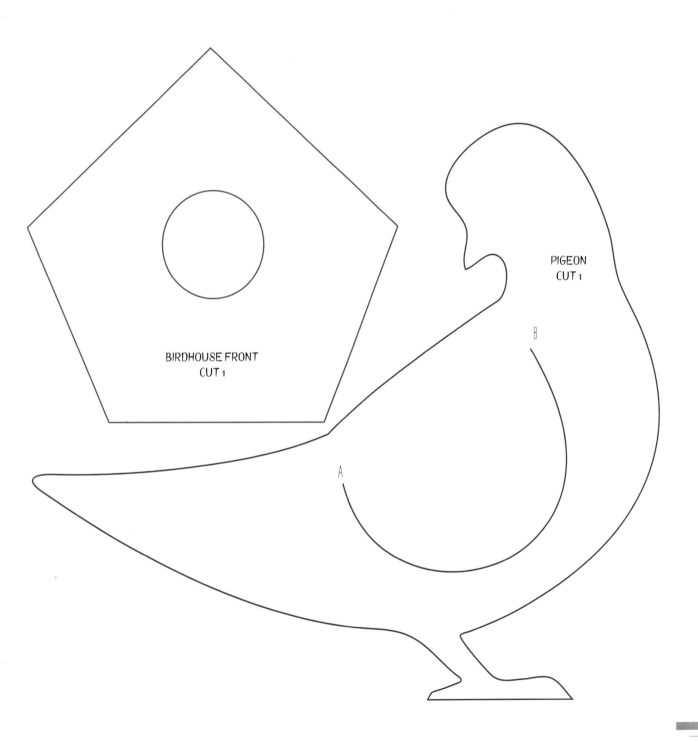

BIRDHOUSE FRONT
CUT 1

PIGEON
CUT 1

B

A

BIRDCAGE POP-UP CARD

Page 32

These templates are actual size.

—— cut   – – – fold

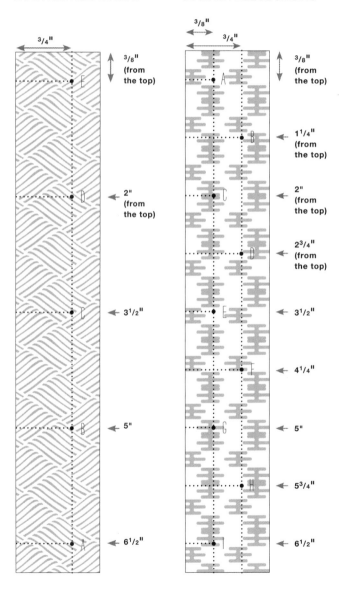

A B   BANNER   B A
CUT 1

BIRD 1
CUT 1

BIRD 2
CUT 1

WING 1
CUT 1
PER BIRD

WING 2
CUT 1
PER BIRD

SMALL
AND LARGE
FLOWERS
CUT AS
MANY AS
NEEDED

BIRDCAGE
CUT 2 (1 REVERSED)

JAPANESE-BOUND NOTEBOOKS

Page 38

BOOK WITH RED BINDING

3/4"

← E   3/8"
(from
the top)

← D   2"
(from
the top)

← C   3 1/2"

← B   5"

← A   6 1/2"

BOOK WITH BLUE BINDING

3/8"
3/4"

← A   3/8"
(from
the top)

← B   1 1/4"
(from
the top)

← C   2"
(from
the top)

← D   2 3/4"
(from
the top)

← E   3 1/2"

← F   4 1/4"

← G   5"

← H   5 3/4"

← I   6 1/2"

BOOK WITH BROWN BINDING

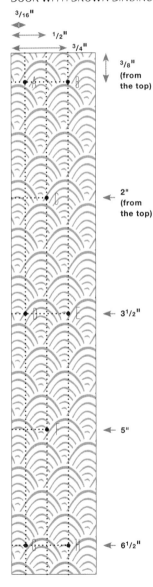

TO MAKE THE BOOK WITH
BLUE BINDING

Follow steps 1–5 for the basic book block
but refer to the binding guide for the blue
book when marking out the drill holes.
Thread the needle with the twine and
starting at the top of the book begin binding.

1. Enter hole A from the rear of the book, take
the twine around the spine of the book and
back into hole A from the rear.

2. Enter hole B from the front of the book,
take the twine around the spine of the book
and back into hole B from the front.

3. Enter hole C from the rear of the book, take
the twine around the spine and back into
hole C from the rear.

4. Enter hole D from the front of the book,
take the twine around the spine and back
into hole D from the front.

5. Enter hole E from the rear of the book, take
the twine around the spine and back into
hole E from the rear.

6. Continue this process until you reach hole I
(when you should be coming from the rear).
Wrap the twine around the spine then travel
back up the book, filling in the missing
stitches. Tie a knot in the twine between
holes A and B and neatly trim the ends.

TO MAKE THE BOOK WITH
BROWN BINDING

Follow steps 1–5 for the basic book block
but refer to the binding guide for the brown
book when marking out the drill holes. You
may want to make the drill holes slightly
larger as the needle does pass through
each hole a few times. Thread the needle
with the twine and starting at the top of the
book begin binding.

1. Enter hole A from the rear of the book, take
the twine around the spine and back into
hole A from the rear.

2. Enter hole C from the front of the book,
take the twine around the spine and back
into hole C from the front.

3. Enter hole D from the rear of the book, take
the twine around the spine and back into
hole D from the rear.

4. Enter hole F from the front of the book, take
the twine around the spine and back into
hole F from the front.

5. Enter hole G from the rear of the book, take
the twine around the spine and back into
hole G from the rear.

6. Enter hole H from the front of the book,
take the needle and twine up to F entering
from the rear.

7. Enter hole E from the front of the book,
come out at hole C entering from the rear.

8. Enter hole B from the front of the book,
come out at hole A entering from the rear.

9. Enter back into hole B from the front then
out at hole C entering from the rear.

10. Enter hole E from the front then out at hole
F entering from the rear.

11. Enter hole H from the front then across to
hole G entering from the rear.

12. Enter hole F from the front then up to hole
D entering from the rear.

13. Enter hole C from the front then tie the
threads together between holes A and C at
the back of the book.

ANEMONE AND CAMELLIA BOUQUET

Page 46
These templates are actual size.
—— cut

ANEMONE PETAL
CUT 1 TO USE AS
A TEMPLATE

CAMELLIA PETAL 1
CUT 1 TO USE AS
A TEMPLATE

CAMELLIA PETAL 2
CUT 1 TO USE AS
A TEMPLATE

CAMELLIA PETAL 3
CUT 1 TO USE AS
A TEMPLATE

FLORAL GIFT BOX GARLAND

Page 50
These templates are actual size.
—— cut --- fold

LEAVES
CUT AS MANY
AS NEEDED

ROSE LEAF
CUT 2 PER
FLOWER

DAISY LEAF
CUT 3 PER FLOWER

SMALL
PASSION
FLOWER
CUT 1

DAISY FLOWER
CUT 1 OF EACH
SHAPE

A
C
B
D

PETALS
CUT AS
MANY AS
NEEDED IN
EACH SIZE

LARGE
PASSION
FLOWER
CUT 1

ROSE, PASSION FLOWER & DAISY GIFT TAGS

Page 54–58
These templates have been scaled down to fit on
the page. To use the template, simply photocopy
the sample at 200%.
—— cut --- fold

CUT AWAY
BLUE AREA
OF EYES

HAREBELL PETAL
CUT 1
TO USE AS
A TEMPLATE

OWL GIFT BOX
CUT 1 PER GIFT BOX

GIANT HAREBELL STRING OF LIGHTS

Page 64
This template is actual size.
—— cut

OWL GIFT BOXES

Page 60
These templates have been scaled
down to fit on the page. To use the
template, simply photocopy the
sample at 200%.
—— cut – – – fold

OWL GIFT BOX INSERT
CUT 1 PER GIFT BOX

WATERLILY TABLE CENTERPIECE

Page 72
These templates have been scaled down to fit on the
page. To use the template, simply photocopy
the sample at 200%
—— cut
– – – fold.

SMALL
PETALS
CUT 2 PER
FLOWER

LARGE PETALS
CUT 2 PER FLOWER

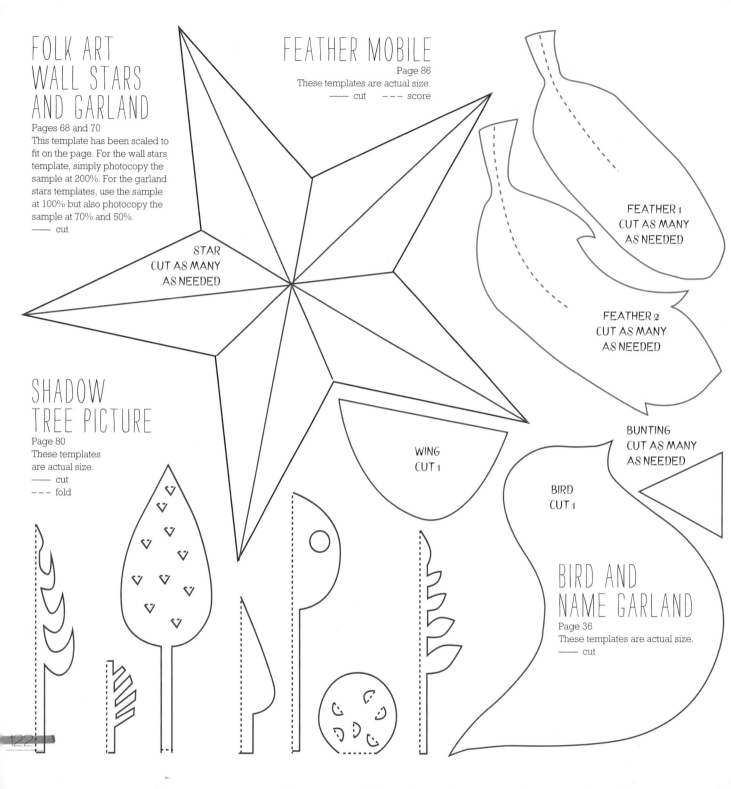

FOLK ART WALL STARS AND GARLAND

Pages 68 and 70
This template has been scaled to fit on the page. For the wall stars template, simply photocopy the sample at 200%. For the garland stars templates, use the sample at 100% but also photocopy the sample at 70% and 50%.
—— cut

STAR
CUT AS MANY
AS NEEDED

FEATHER MOBILE

Page 86
These templates are actual size.
—— cut   – – – score

FEATHER 1
CUT AS MANY
AS NEEDED

FEATHER 2
CUT AS MANY
AS NEEDED

SHADOW TREE PICTURE

Page 80
These templates are actual size.
—— cut
– – – fold

WING
CUT 1

BIRD
CUT 1

BUNTING
CUT AS MANY
AS NEEDED

BIRD AND NAME GARLAND

Page 36
These templates are actual size.
—— cut

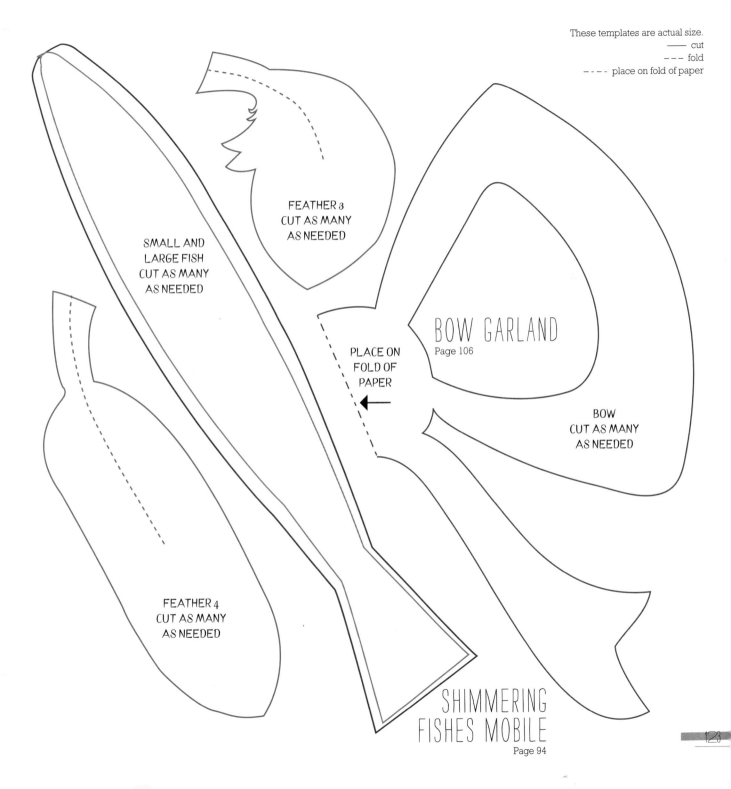

These templates are actual size.
——— cut
– – – fold
- - - - place on fold of paper

FEATHER 3
CUT AS MANY
AS NEEDED

SMALL AND
LARGE FISH
CUT AS MANY
AS NEEDED

BOW GARLAND
Page 106

PLACE ON
FOLD OF
PAPER

BOW
CUT AS MANY
AS NEEDED

FEATHER 4
CUT AS MANY
AS NEEDED

SHIMMERING
FISHES MOBILE
Page 94

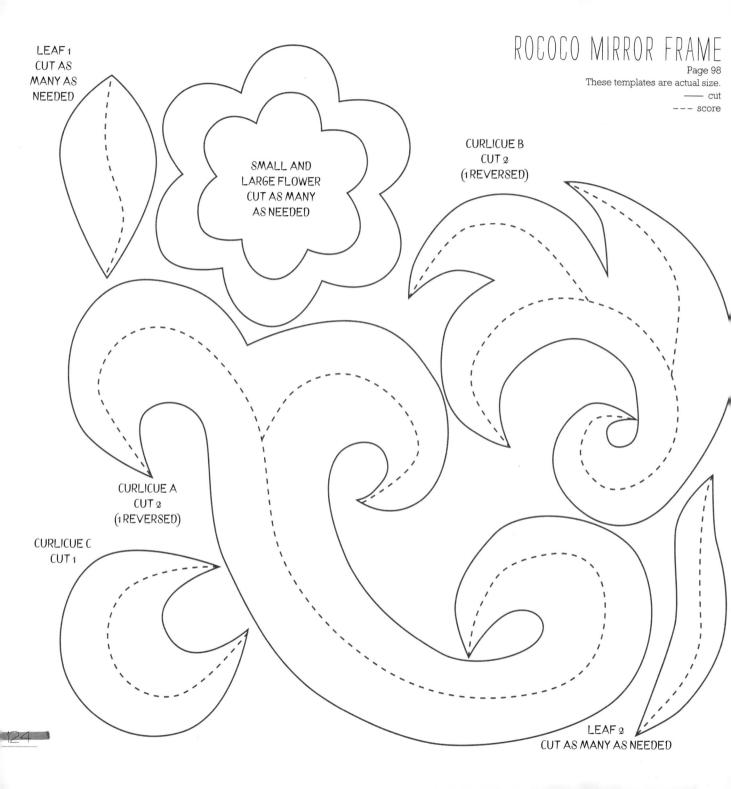

LEAF 1
CUT AS
MANY AS
NEEDED

SMALL AND
LARGE FLOWER
CUT AS MANY
AS NEEDED

CURLICUE B
CUT 2
(1 REVERSED)

CURLICUE A
CUT 2
(1 REVERSED)

CURLICUE C
CUT 1

LEAF 2
CUT AS MANY AS NEEDED

THE AMAZING AERIAL ACROBATS

Page 110
These templates have been scaled down to fit on the page.
To use the template, simply
photocopy the sample
at 200%.
—— cut

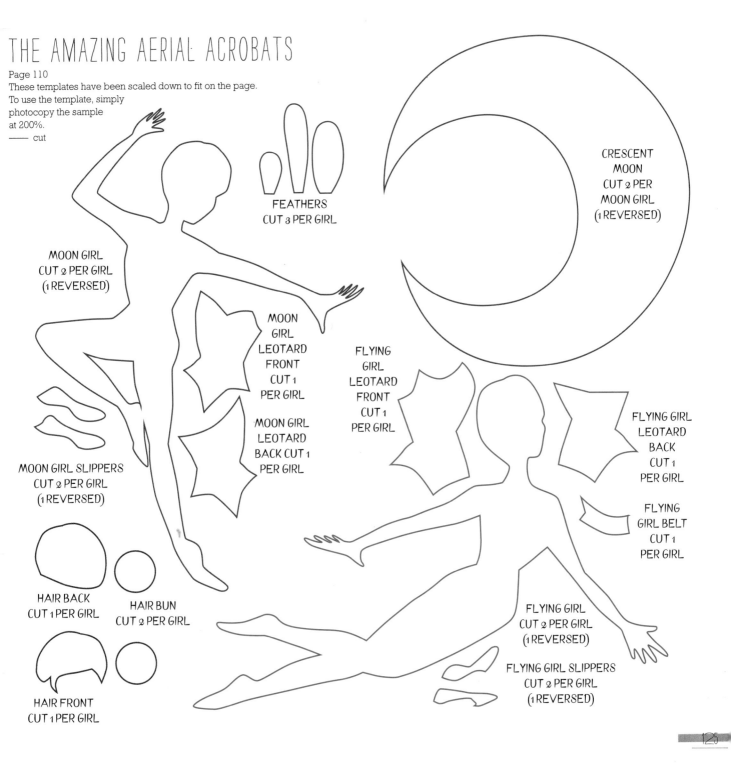

FEATHERS
CUT 3 PER GIRL

CRESCENT
MOON
CUT 2 PER
MOON GIRL
(1 REVERSED)

MOON GIRL
CUT 2 PER GIRL
(1 REVERSED)

MOON
GIRL
LEOTARD
FRONT
CUT 1
PER GIRL

MOON GIRL
LEOTARD
BACK CUT 1
PER GIRL

FLYING
GIRL
LEOTARD
FRONT
CUT 1
PER GIRL

FLYING GIRL
LEOTARD
BACK
CUT 1
PER GIRL

MOON GIRL SLIPPERS
CUT 2 PER GIRL
(1 REVERSED)

FLYING
GIRL BELT
CUT 1
PER GIRL

HAIR BACK
CUT 1 PER GIRL

HAIR BUN
CUT 2 PER GIRL

FLYING GIRL
CUT 2 PER GIRL
(1 REVERSED)

FLYING GIRL SLIPPERS
CUT 2 PER GIRL
(1 REVERSED)

HAIR FRONT
CUT 1 PER GIRL

RESOURCES

All my craft materials and tools come from the following stores and websites. You can find your own supplies at your local online sites and craft stores.

US SUPPLIERS

A.C. MOORE
acmoore.com

JOANN'S FABRICS AND CRAFTS
www.joann.com

MICHAEL'S FABRIC STORE
www.michaels.com

UK SUPPLIERS

ARJOWIGGINS CREATIVE PAPERS
arjowigginscreativepapers.com
Great website full of inspiration.

ARTBOX
artbox.co.uk
Cute Japanese stationery, notebooks, erasers, and stickers.

BLADE RUBBER
bladerubberstamps.co.uk
A beautiful shop choc-full of stamps, inks, and scrapbooking supplies.

COWLING AND WILCOX
cowlingandwilcox.com
Large art shop with five London branches.

FREE ONLINE FONTS
There are lots of websites with free fonts to download. For starters, try …
dafont.com or fontsquirrel.com

HOBBYCRAFT
hobbycraft.co.uk
A hobby and craft superstore.

ELLA JOHNSTON
ellajohnston.wordpress.com
Beautiful art and illustration, and supplier of the bird pictures featured in this book.

LIBERTY
liberty.co.uk
Regent Street, London W1B 5AH
Shop with an inspiring stationery department.

MUJI
muji.com
A good place for small metal rulers and Perspex storage solutions that are great for keeping your papers organized.

PAPERCHASE
paperchase.co.uk
213–215 Tottenham Court Road
London W1T 7PS
The London flagship store on Tottenham Court Road has so many papers it's ridiculous. Also sells lovely stationery.

PRESENT AND CORRECT
presentandcorrect.com
23 Arlington Way, London EC1R 1UY
The shop and online store that feeds my printed paper addiction. This is where to buy vintage German sausage packaging and old exercise books.

PULLINGERS ART SHOP
pullingers.com
Good online art suppliers.

RAINBOW FLORIST SUPPLIES
rainbowfloristsupplies.co.uk
Crepe paper and other floristry goodies.

RYMAN
ryman.co.uk
The place for office supplies like hole reinforcers and gold stars.

G.F. SMITH
gfsmith.com
Paper suppliers offering lots of helpful tips on choosing the right paper for your project. Also provides samples.

TASHTORI ARTS AND CRAFTS
facebook.com/pages/TashTori-Arts-and-Crafts/214629638549591
Art shop with good paper and scrapbooking supplies.

WASHI TAPES
washitapes.co.uk
For all your washi tape needs.

INDEX

THANK YOU, THANK YOU, THANK YOU

Thanks to all at Quadrille, especially Lisa, Claire, and Chinh. And thank you to Hilary and Gemma for making the book make sense and look beautiful.

To lovely Keiko for more amazing photography, calmness, and general patience.

To all my family, Mum for her general brilliance, Dad for his remarkable prop making, Jo for her paper skills suggestions, Ian and the boys always inspiring me with their handmade cards and gifts, Auntie and Uncle, Nanny and Grandad for their support, belief, encouragement, and suggestions.

Thank you Elias and Barry for allowing me a supermarket sweep for props from your inspiring home.

Love to Jake, Kirsty, Laura, Hannah (both of them) for listening to my ramblings, half-finished sentences, and general maniacal behavior.

To Rhiannon, who knew that when we had our little stall at the school craft fair it would lead to this?!

Publishing Director Jane O'Shea
Commissioning Editor Lisa Pendreigh
Editor Hilary Mandleberg
Creative Director Helen Lewis
Art Direction & Design Claire Peters
Designer Gemma Wilson
Photographer Keiko Oikawa
Stylist and Illustrator Christine Leech
Production Director Vincent Smith
Production Controller Aysun Hughes

First edition for the
United States and Canada
published in 2014 by
Barron's Educational Series, Inc.

Text, project designs, artwork & illustrations
© 2013 Christine Leech
Photography
© 2013 Keiko Oikawa
Design & layout
© 2013 Quadrille Publishing Ltd.

First published in 2013 by
Quadrille Publishing Ltd.
Alhambra House
27–31 Charing Cross Road
London WC2H 0LS
www.quadrille.co.uk

The designs in this book are
copyright and must not be
made for resale.

The rights of Christine Leech to be identified as the author of this work have been asserted by her in accordance with the Copyright, Design, and Patents Act 1988.

All inquiries should be addressed to:
Barron's Educational Series, Inc.
250 Wireless Boulevard
Hauppauge, NY 11788
www.barronseduc.com

ISBN: 978-1-4380-0470-9
Library of Congress Control No.: 2014938262

9 8 7 6 5 4 3 2 1

Printed in China